GW00494426

COCKER SPANIEL HANDBOOK

Be Gays Twinkle and Shine
sire: Be Gays Bullwinkle
dam: Be Gay Zippitidoda
Owners, Bill Ernst and Elizabeth Coons.

the

COCKER SPANIEL HANDBOOK

by

Ernest H. Hart

Drawings by the Author

ISBN 0-87666-270-X

Distributed in the UNITED STATES by T.F.H. Publications, Inc., One T.F.H. Plaza, Neptune City, NJ 07753; in CANADA to the Pet Trade by H & L Pet Supplies Inc., 27 Kingston Crescent, Kitchener, Ontario N2B 2T6; Rolf C. Hagen Ltd., 3225 Sartelon Street, Montreal 382 Quebec; in CANADA to the Book Trade by Macmillan of Canada (A Division of Canada Publishing Corporation), 164 Commander Boulevard, Agincourt, Ontario M1S 3C7; in ENGLAND by T.F.H. Publications Limited, Cliveden House/Priors Way/Bray, Maidenhead, Berkshire SL6 2HP, England; in AUSTRALIA AND THE SOUTH PACIFIC by T.F.H. (Australia) Pty. Ltd., Box 149, Brookvale 2100 N.S.W., Australia; in NEW ZEALAND by Ross Haines & Son, Ltd., 82 D Elizabeth Knox Place, Panmure, Auckland, New Zealand; in the PHILIPPINES by Bio-Research, 5 Lippay Street, San Lorenzo Village, Makati Rizal; in SOUTH AFRICA by Multipet Pty. Ltd., Box 235 New Germany, South Africa 3620. Published by T.F.H. Publications, Inc. Manufactured in the United States of America by T.F.H. Publications, Inc.

To my mother and father,

who gave to me and fostered
my love of animals,
particularly dogs.

cover painting by Ernest H. Hart

photography by: Gunderson, Frasie, Bennett Associates, Stephen Klein, Ardslae Studio, Wm. P. Gilbert, Norton of Kent, International News, Wm. Brown, Ritter, Tauskey, Johnnie McMillan, Deopaul, George Pickow (Three Lions, Inc.), Louise Van der Meid, Percy Jones, Romaine, Wm. L. Glover, Norman, Bill Day, Joan Ludwig, Liz, Evelyn M. Shafer, and Devlin Photo Service.

Contents

Foreword

The author has long believed that the Cocker Spaniel is the finest small breed of dog ever evolved for the benefit of mankind. I am sure that anyone who has ever owned or shot over a Cocker will agree. The fact that the breed has slipped down from the heights in numerical supremacy is, in my opinion, a good and healthy thing. Any breed that stays too long at the top in numbers registered by the AKC attracts undesirable people who are quick to leech what they can financially from the breed's popularity without a thought for the good of the breed genetically.

To write this book has not been an easy task, though writing is my business along with painting and illustrating. There have been, over the years, a few breeds of the many with which I have been associated, that I have particularly liked and admired. The Cocker is one of those breeds. Because of this warmth that I have for the breed, writing this book, though not as I have said, an easy task, has certainly been a gratifying one. You who read it and, I hope, enjoy and benefit from it, can have no idea of the tremendous accumulation of data amassed, read, sifted and selected from. It was necessary to spend much time in study and critical appraisal to separate true fact from mere opinion, for opinion can be had anywhere for the asking but fact is hard to come by. It was difficult, in many instances, for me to be completely objective and resist coloring fact from experience. Yet experience in knowing hands has its own value and has been employed where it paralleled fact.

I have particularly attempted to anticipate your every need, your every question in regard to the breed of your choice, and present the answers in a fashion which you will understand and enjoy reading. I know that some of you will disagree with certain precepts and concepts within these covers which are contrary to your own experience and belief. That is as it should be, for no man is perfect, no book written by man is the complete and end answer, and intelligent argument is ever the basis for new thought, theory and improvement.

If I have succeeded in bringing to you a more comprehensive picture of the Cocker and the many facets of his use and care, in some parts or portion of this book, it is perhaps, because I have written it in Spain, the country where the ancestors of the Cocker, in fact the forebears of all Spaniels, had their earliest beginnings.

To those of you who have graciously allowed my publisher to print requested photographs of specific dogs, and to all those learned people listed in the bibliography from whom I have selected and borrowed the results of years of research and accumulated knowledge to give to you, I offer thanks.

Torremolinos,
Spain

ERNEST H. HART

7

The fine silver buff dog, Ch. Juniper's Just Snowed, Best of Variety at the 1965 New England Cocker Spaniel Breeeders Club. Owned by Mrs. Ina S. Ginsberg, handled by Ted Young, Jr.

I

Genealogy of the Cocker Spaniel

The Spaniel family is of ancient lineage and usefulness to mankind. The fact that the Spaniels are still a widespread and admired group of dogs at the present time is proof of their value in the past for man was, at an earlier time, ruthless in his selection of canine companions. Those that were not particularly and pertinently efficient were eliminated as being unfit to share man's star-crossed destiny. Thus arbitrary but very effective selection shaped the evolutionary pattern of the familiar breeds of the canine species and one of the categories chosen for survival was the spaniel clan.

THE DOG IN PREHISTORY

A long time ago, before the apelike creature that was to provide the amazing evolutionary basis for *Homo sapiens* swung down from the trees into the path of social significance, a four-footed creature roamed the earth that was of the mammalian stock from which would eventually evolve cats, hyenas, seals, bears, raccoons and dogs. Time passed and ancient ages moved in the miasmic mists of far prehistory back to extinction. Animals emerged from the far away fog of early life, species that possessed genetic elasticity, the ability to foster and harbor mutation against environmental modification and so to continue to exist as a species despite drastic change. One such animal that survived the ages was *Tomarctus*, the prototype canine that roamed the rugged, still forming earth about fifteen million years ago.

Short-legged, quick, predatory, Tomarctus was the ancestor of the foxes, the wolves and coyotes as well as the wild dogs of the world and our own, now domesticated, *Canis familiaris*.

With Tomarctus as a genetic basis, there eventually appeared four major prototype canines from which evolved the basic animals destined to form all the known, modern breeds of dogs that would be molded by the vagaries and needs of man to fit his pleasure and purpose. Of these four prototypes we are interested essentially in one, *Canis familiaris intermedius*, for this ancient ancestor lent his germ plasm to the fashioning of a group of rugged, even-tempered hunting and working dogs among which we find the initial spaniels.

EVOLUTION OF THE SPANIEL FAMILY

There are spaniels mentioned in literature written as early as 1386 (called "spaynel" by Chaucer), and by the 15th Century, spaniels were being used to flush the game in falconry. The name of this type of hunting dog points, rather pertinently, to the country of its origin and early development, Spain. In Spain, and in neighboring Portugal, Spanish Spaniels and the basic Spanish Pointer were used in the hunting field by sport-conscious aristocrats. Inevitably, crosses were made between the two breeds which eventually resulted in another group of fine sporting dogs, the setters.

The author has searched Spain diligently in an attempt to find specimens of these important, basic Spanish breeds. There are still some of the native Pointers to be found, not many, but a few, bred by dog-conscious Spanish fanciers in an attempt to keep the breed from extinction. But the Spaniels of Spain seem to have vanished since the Civil War of 1936–1939.

Other countries adopted the early Spanish Spaniel and type began to diversify according to environment, terrain and the needs of the people who

The first true canine, Tomarctus, was long, low to the ground and sported a heavy, long tail. Tomarctus was the prototype dog that was the direct ancestor of the family Canidae that included wolves, foxes, coyotes, and jackals.

kept the breed. Particularly in England did this occur where selection was made for various types and sizes of spaniels and there eventually evolved large, medium and small spaniels. These early dogs began to specialize and were soon divided into three categories, two for land and one for water hunting. There was the "flushing" spaniel that put up game for the falcon or started prey for the coursing hounds; the spaniel that located game and then crouched or "set" before it until the net with which the game was taken had been thrown (often over both dog and game); and the "water" Spaniels, a branch of the family utilized for the hunting and retrieving of game in water. Though there was much crossing of the various developing spaniel breeds, we are primarily interested in the "flushing" type, for it is from this group of animals that the Cocker Spaniel came into being.

From the Pyrame and the Spanish Spaniels came the Field Spaniel, then the Norfolk and Springer Spaniels in turn, and from the Springer was developed the English Cocker Spaniel, direct ancestor of the American Cocker Spaniel. These "cocker" or "cocking" Spaniels, used primarily in the hunting of woodcock, snipe and other lowland birds, were bred down in size to be handy, hardy and easily cared for. Indeed, some of those early "cocking" dogs weighed no more than eleven to sixteen pounds. Such small dogs could have had little to recommend them as true gundogs and were probably used as "starters" for coursing dogs. Another branch of this same family developed into other spaniels of the Sussex and Field type. It was not unusual, in those days, to find dogs from the same litter split into two classifications, the smaller ones called Cockers and the larger ones, Field Spaniels. Incidentally during the Cocker's initial introduction to America in the early 1880s, the only distinction between Cockers and Field Spaniels, in the show ring, was one of size. A dog weighing over twenty-eight pounds was considered a Field Spaniel, and if under this weight he would be classified as a Cocker. It has been reported that occasionally, at early dog shows, an animal of good type kept thin, could win as a Cocker in the morning and, after a hearty meal, compete later in the day in Field Spaniel classes. A third line of small spaniels developed which were bred away from usefulness toward extreme dwarfism and became, in time, the Toy Spaniels.

Rather wide and unorganized classification continued until the middle of the 19th Century and it was not until 1883 that classes for Cockers were listed in English shows. A year before this, in 1882, a large black spaniel weighing about forty pounds, had been shown at the Westminster Show in New York. There was some controversy over the dog's listing, whether it should be as a Cocker or some other spaniel breed. He was finally classified and shown as a Field Spaniel.

Meanwhile, in 1893, the Kennel Club (England) accepted the Cocker Spaniel as a definite breed and granted it entrance to the Stud Book. This official recognition separated the Cocker from all other Spaniels as a specific type so that no longer could other breeds of Spaniels, even though hunted on woodcock, be called "cocker" or "cocking" Spaniels.

THE COCKER SPANIEL IN AMERICA

In America Cocker Spaniels had been exhibited in show classes before the American Kennel Club was organized in 1884. Those early Cockers, seen in shows in both England and America, were mostly parti-colored or, if solids, were various shades of tan or red. In 1882 the American Spaniel Club was organized. Up to that time there had been only one type of Cocker Spaniel visualized by the breeders but, with the founding of this new club dedicated to the Cocker, the English and the American Cockers began to diverge in type. The English Cocker was developed as more of a "Setter" type Spaniel, while the American breed held to the general appearance of

The large, rough, Water Dog or Water Spaniel, used for hunting and retrieving game in water. From an old English woodcut (Thomas Bewick).

the basic Cocker Spaniel progenitors but became more cobby in body and sported a stronger and more distinctive head.

Under the guidance of men like James Watson and the Canadian fancier George D. MacDougal (both of the American breed club in New York), the American Cocker became more and more unlike his English cousin. As time passed, this difference in breed type became increasingly apparent, yet Cockers, English and American, were still linked together in show classifications and had to compete against each other in the same classes. Finally, in 1949, the American Kennel Club, after prolonged efforts by breeders and specialty clubs of both Cocker types, granted them separate recognition as distinct and individual breeds. The American Cocker Spaniel, the smallest of the sporting breeds, had come into its own and soon skyrocketed to the heights it deserved to become the most popular breed in the vast aristocracy of dogdom.

*The basic type of Spanish Pointer (above),
crossed with the old Spaniels of Spain, eventually
resulted in another fine group of sporting dogs,
the Setters (below).*

*The earliest Cocker Spaniels were mostly
parti-colored like this top winning modern black
and white parti, Ch. Fraclin Colonel Caridas,
owned by Edward Boehm. He was best in the
Sporting Group at Westminster in 1962 and is
shown here winning Best Sporting at the Ashville
K.C. Show under judge Marie Meyer, ably
handled by Ted Young, Jr.*

II

Early History of the Cocker Spaniel

PILLARS OF THE BREED

Up to and including the present day the history of the American Cocker Spaniel has been formed by three dramatic segments, each marked by the birth and genetic fulfillment of a specific stud dog who brought to the breed a new concept of type and, through extraordinary prepotency, helped fix that visualized mold in succeeding generations. Each of these animals was, without doubt, a fortuitous type mutant who arrived at a time when their worth would be luckily recognized and utilized to carry the breed a giant step forward.

The first of these important dogs resulted from the importation of a bred bitch, Chloe II, by Mr. F. F. Pitcher. She had been whelped in England by a Mr. Bullock and the sire of the litter she carried in utero to the United States was Obo, owned by Mr. Farrow and registered with the English Kennel Club as being "by Fred and out of Betty". *In Dalziell's *British Dogs*, Obo is described as being of the following size and measurements: Weight—22 pounds, Height—10 inches, Length from nose to occiput—$7\frac{1}{4}$ inches, Length from nose to eyes—$2\frac{1}{4}$ inches, Length from nose to set on of tail—29 inches.

In the litter which Chloe II subsequently whelped on August 7, 1882, there was a fine black puppy male which was registered as Obo II, A.K.C. registration number 4911, and was sold to a Mr. J. P. Willey. Upon reaching maturity Obo II proved to be nothing less than sensational. This great dog

---

*AUTHOR'S NOTE: Though this description is supposed to be of Obo, sire of Obo II, the author is of the opinion that it is instead a description of Obo II, the closeness of the names of sire and son causing the mistake.

standardized and became the foundation sire of the American Cocker Spaniel.

Obo II sired large litters and, in a time when most Cockers were (or carried and so passed on) particolor, red or liver, he begat a great many solid black puppies. He made his championship in September, 1883, at the Lowell, Massachusetts show, three months after he had been started on his campaign. He was far ahead of any male cocker of his era as either a show dog or sire. Mason, author of *Our Prize Dogs*, shrewdly and critically assessed Obo II as follows: "Skull showing slight coarseness. Muzzle should be deeper, with a cleaner-cut appearance in every direction; it is wider than we like and the lower incisors project slightly. Ears correct in size, shape, position, quality, and carriage. Eyes good in color, size, and expression. Neck somewhat too heavy. Chest deep, with ribs beautifully sprung. Shoulders strong and free. Back firm. Loin compact and strong. Hindquarters of exquisite formation. Forelegs showing great strength and set into good feet. Stern well set. Carriage gay. Coat showing slight curliness, especially on neck and hindquarters. Feather profuse. A thick-set and sturdy little dog that looks exactly what he is—the prince of stud dogs—his worth to the Cocker interests of this country cannot be overestimated." James Watson praised Obo II without abstention, summing up his critique, ". . . he is a long way in front of any of his sex in this country so far, either as a show dog or sire."

Premier, considered by some authorities to be the greatest foundation sire in the breed. Whelped in 1896 he was bred and owned by George Douglas.
sire: Black Duke   dam: Woodland Flossie

The great Obo II, whelped in 1882.
sire: Obo   dam: Chloe II

*Black Duke, famous son of Obo II, was thought
to be the greatest sire after his father.*

17

Some of the best Cockers of the day were in the Toronto (owned or bred by Mr. MacDougal) and the Massachusetts areas. Bitches from this stock were bred to Obo II and these matings resulted in the subsequent production of such great foundation animals as, Miss Obo, King of Obo, Little Red Rover, Betty Obo, Ted Obo, Frank Obo, Minnie Obo, Tim and Lily Obo. Other great animals, either directly sired by Obo II or closely related to him were, Jersey, Doc, Red Doc, Dunrobin, Beatrice W., Helen, La Tosca, Juno W., Shina, Darkie, Brant, Ann Obo, Bambo, Bonnie of En Chanto, Black Pete, Bobby, Goldstream Friar Tuck, Hornell Silk, I Say, Middy, Midkiff Demonstrator, Miss Obo II, and the great Black Duke. These animals, combined with other good, available stock, particularly Braeside breeding, set the standard for the American Cocker.

Following Obo II, his son, Black Duke, whelped in 1896, became the greatest sire of his generation. This dog was owned and bred by James Luckwell and was out of Woodland Queen. Baby Ruth was another great Cocker, a bitch, of that era. She was whelped in 1892, was bred by W. Barclay, owned by Mepal Kennels, and was the proud possessor of the most classical headpiece up to her time. Her sire was My Joe, and her dam, Fascination. Premier, a fine son of Black Duke out of Woodland Flossie, bred and owned by George Douglas, in turn sired Premio out of Lubra, the latter bitch owned by O. B. Gilman, and Premio became the foundation of the Gilman's famous Idahurst Kennels.

The author well remembers that fine gentleman, Mr. Gilman and his sweet and gentle wife. I visited with them and, at their request, spoke before their Cocker club several times. That was a long time ago but I still look back with quiet and sincere pleasure to the moments I spent with those fine people and their friends in the Cocker fancy. Subsequently I owned several of the Idahurst Cockers, sweet and lovely animals that were a delight to live with.

Idahurst Belle and Idahurst Roderic were only two of the many great Cockers produced by the Gilman Kennels. Meanwhile Mepal Kennels, owned by Mr. Bloodgood, came into focus in the show ring as did Brookside and Mount Vernon Kennels and the Belle Isle Kennels, owned by Mrs. Warner. Mr. William T. Payne successfully exhibited fine parti-colors, while on the Pacific coast Governor James Rolph of California founded the Mission Kennels with the blue roan bitch, Beechgrove Topsy. Fine animals from this kennel provided foundation stock for many of the important Cocker kennels on the coast during that era. Other important strains established on the coast in the very early part of the 20th Century were Denniston, Golden Gate, Bellmore and Knebworth. The breed was in a healthy state and the stage was set for the second dramatic act in the story of the American Cocker.

The curtain was raised by the hand of one of the greatest Cocker Spaniel breeders of all time, Herman E. Mellenthin. In his soon-to-be-famous My

Partis of the Past.

Right: Ch. Overcross Pepper, 1912. By Idahurst Beau x Overcross Nora. Center: Ch. Denniston Nugget, 1911. By Mepals Olaf x Denniston Lady Margaret. Below: Ch. Idahurst Belle II, 1928. O.B. Gilman's great bitch, by Robinhurst Muffedit x Idahurst Charm.

The great Red Brucie. Bred by Herman E. Mellenthin, this famous mutant failed to become a champion, yet his prepotency as a stud dog has become legend.

Ch, Midkiff Miracle Man shared the same sire as Red Brucie. His dam was Midkiff Seductive.

Own Kennels, a little red puppy had been born in a litter by Robinhurst Foreglow and out of Ree's Dolly. Mellenthin was one of those few people blessed with an inborn, instinctive "dog sense" and an "eye for a good 'un," even in the nest. He saw that "good 'un" in the bold, little red puppy in the whelping box.

The puppy was an exaggeration of everything a good Cocker puppy should be and his breeder refused to sell him claiming, with amazing foresight, that the red pup would become the greatest stud dog the breed had ever known. Mr. Mellenthin did not, at that time, have a registered kennel name and he wanted the red pup to be named Red Bruce. But the American Kennel Club changed the name slightly (a permissible privilege) and the dog was instead registered as Red Brucie.

At maturity Red Brucie was still so overdone in many of the characteristics breeders were striving for that he was ahead of his time. As a matter of fact and record his show career was much less than impressive and he never made his championship. But this was one dog who didn't have to have the generally important prefix "Champion" to lure bitches to his stud stall. With the help of his breeder and subsequently his own record, he was recognized for what he was, the greatest stud force in Cocker history up to his time.

Descriptions of Red Brucie run almost exactly parallel to those of Obo II before him except for the relation of length to height, for Brucie was high stationed and short in back. He possessed a very strong head and heavy bone. He was prepotent in passing to his get this unprecedented short back which, combined with the longer legs, produced an admired high-stationed cobbiness. He also stamped his progeny with his long neck set beautifully into lean, sloping, well angulated shoulders, along with a driving, coordinated gait, the gift of his superb balance. I might mention here that Red Brucie's sire, Robinhurst Foreglow, was of the same type as his famous son but not quite as exaggerated in degree.

Red Brucie's initial outstanding accomplishment that marked him as a great sire, was the production of the "Big Four" litter. Bred to a beautiful black bitch, Champion Princess Marie, the subsequent litter, whelped in 1922, consisted of four of the greatest Cockers of the day, Champion My Own Straight Sale, Champion My Own Peter Manning, Champion My Own Desire, and Champion My Own Rowcliffe Princess. These animals, three of which were sold, became foundation stock in the creation of solid colored Cockers for Windsweep Kennels (founding a great line of blacks for Miss Dodsworth), Rowcliffe Kennels, and Sandspring Kennels. Though of most importance in solid colors, Red Brucie, through his son Champion Rowcliffe Red Man and several other fine animals, was also of considerable influence in producing fine parti-colors.

Brucie was just past a year old when the "Big Four" litter was whelped.

The result was, of course, that everyone wanted to breed their Cocker bitch to Red Brucie, and most of them did, for there had never been a stud dog of any breed in such public demand as was Red Brucie. It didn't hinder his career as a stud either when in 1927 the good bitch, Sweet Georgia Brown, owned by Thomas Carleton, produced a litter by Red Brucie which resulted in five more champions. His great son, My Own Brucie, was twice best in show at the Westminster Kennel Club Show in New York City.

The records prove that Mr. Mellenthin's prediction of his red dog's genetic worth was no guess. Red Brucie sired thirty-four champions and many fine animals that didn't make their championships for one reason or another, but who proved their worth in the breeding pen. Red Brucie was still giving of his own greatness to his progeny when he was thirteen years of age. The week before he died, at thirteen, Red Brucie was bred to seven bitches all of whom produced fine litters by the immortal stud. His influence on the breed is almost immeasurable for his genetic value carried on from one generation to the next like a stone dropped into a placid pool spreading ripples outward in ever widening circles.

PEDIGREE OF RED BRUCIE

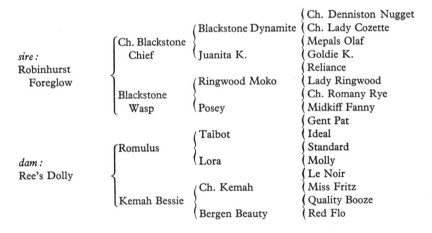

The third dog to greatly influence the breed and stamp type in the modern show Cocker was the great black champion, Torohill Trader, whelped in 1932 and owned by Leonard J. Buck, owner also of The Great My Own and My Own Backwoodsman among other fine dogs. Torohill Trader was by Torohill Trouper and out of Torohill Tidy and was again a slight departure in type from the existing standard toward an envisioned ideal. Trader was a square dog, short in back, up in the legs, long in neck with a beautiful head

*Ch. Princess Marie, by Lucky Durbar x Gold
Girl, was the dam of the "Big Four" litter,
by Red Brucie.*

*Below, Ch. My Own Today was
sired by one of the "Big Four" litter, My Own
Peter Manning x My Own Prudence.*

Ch. Torohill Trader, 1932.

He was great as both a producer and show dog. Leonard J. Buck's famous black set a new type standard in the breed.
sire: Torohill Trouper   dam: Torohill Tidy

and he was, overall, a larger dog than his male contemporaries and possessed heavier furnishings of great density. The different nuances of type which were his heritage and which he passed on to his progeny became fixed in the breed and this eventually led to changes in the standard of the Cocker.

That Torohill Trader was a great dog in the grand tradition of Obo II and Red Brucie cannot be denied and is proven by his record as a stud and show dog. Starting in 1934 at the Morris and Essex show, Torohill Trader won best of breed in the largest breed entry ever exhibited in a one-day, outdoor show in this country up to that date. It was also the largest breed entry of the show. In that year he was best of breed fourteen times, won three sporting groups, and was twice best in show. The following year, 1935, he was best of breed eighteen times, ten times a group winner and six times best in show. The next year he won fifteen bests of breed, seven sporting groups, and was once best in show all breeds. Shown only twice in '37, this great dog was best in show at the American Spaniel Club specialty show, and entered in the stud dog class only at Boston, won handily.

Among his most prominent get were the notable winners and producers; Nonquitt Notable, 1937 winner of the A.K.C. certificate for the leading winner amongst sporting dogs; Torohill Smokey, who won the sporting group and best American-bred in show at Westminster in 1937, also other top wins at Detroit, Cornwall, etc.; Blackstone Reflector who, including many fine wins, took best of breed at the Cocker Spaniel Specialty of Boston in 1937 (192 dogs benched); Blow's Discovery, Orthodox Bagatelle, Belinda

*Ch. Found, a top winner owned by Mrs. Leonard
J. Buck.
sire: My Own Ladysman
dam: My Own Lady Brucie*

Belle of Romarwyn, Baroness of Huntington, and many other greats of the past of like quality were all sired by Torohill Trader.

Three dogs, each one evidently a type mutant and able to stamp their progeny with their own genetic advance toward greater breed beauty. Three dogs whose greatness was luckily recognized and utilized for breed improvement. Who can say how many more there may have been who could have done as much but were unrecognized, unheralded, and left to become

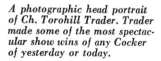

A photographic head portrait of Ch. Torohill Trader. Trader made some of the most spectacular show wins of any Cocker of yesterday or today.

nonentities and of no consequence to the breed. Perhaps one or more, perhaps none. But, we can be greateful that these three Cockers were identified by knowledgeable fanciers and their greatness incorporated into the breed.

The present standard, approved and adopted at the end of 1957, stresses height at the withers and makes no mention of weight. In the early standard for the American Cocker Spaniel no height measurements were included, instead a weight of "Not under 18 nor exceeding 24 pounds" was used as the yardstick of size. Later, with the new "Trader" type appearing, it was realized that this weight allowance was not enough and was not a true indication of correct size.

HISTORY OF THE COCKER SPANIEL IN THE FIELD

Cocker Spaniels were conceived and originally bred to be gun dogs. Though Spaniels known as "cocking" or "cocker" Spaniels were of various hunting Spaniel breeds, Thorburn, in his *Shooting Directory* published in 1805, describes the Cocker Spaniel as differing from other breeds and "esteemed for its compact form. The coat is more inclined to curl like a Springer's and the tail is commonly truncated. The colors are, liver and white, red, red and white, black and white, all liver, and sometimes black with tanned legs and muzzle." This would indicate that as of that date or

Ch. Mepals Ionian, 1921.
Owned by Mrs. Haley Fiske.
sire: *Mepals Minto*   dam: *Lavonia*

before the Cocker Spaniel was a definite breed. But he adds, to the book and to the confusion, "some of the strongest Cockers were found in Sussex and called Sussex Spaniels." Of one thing we can be sure—that the first Cockers to be brought to America from England were imported by hunters to serve as gun dogs.

The first field trials for Spaniels held in Great Britain were sponsored by the Sporting Spaniel Club of England and took place on January 3rd and 4th, 1899. Both stakes were won by a twenty-five pound Cocker Spaniel by the name of Stylish Pride. In 1903 the first trials in England that listed events for Cockers took place and made history for the breed in that country. In 1904 two trials were held for Cockers, in 1913, six trials and in 1918 there were eighteen. By that time forty-six Spaniel Clubs had come into being in England. This latter date is getting a bit ahead of our story but this increasing popularity in England, at that time, certainly reacted favorably for the Cocker in America at a slightly later date, when combined with physical changes in the breed as mentioned shortly in this text.

During the latter part of the 19th Century the Cocker, as a gun dog, lost popularity. The Springer Spaniel came on to take his place with sporting men and the Cocker was banished from the field and thought of as a pet and show dog exclusively and no longer a working member of the sporting dog fraternity. This disposition of the breed by hunters and field trial enthusiasts continued for approximately fifty years. The reason for the decline

Ch. Bellmore Buffkins, 1913, bred by Miss Louise Hering and owned by Miss Mary Connors, was by Denniston's Nugget x Tarbaby from Goldenstate.

of the Cocker in this area which was actually its environment is easily apparent if one will but look at existing photographs of the Cockers of that period. Compare the anatomical proportions of the Cockers with those of the Springer Spaniels that were their contemporaries and you will immediately realize the great advantages the Springer would have in the field. Obo II, the greatest Cocker of his time, was almost nineteen inches longer than he was high!

The faddists had taken a firm grip on the Cocker and bred it to an extreme physically that represented, to them, visual beauty but which made the Cocker less than useful in the field. The breed was long, low-set to the point of exaggeration and, because of these selected for, and inbred, proportions could no longer compete with other Spaniels in the job for which the breed had been conceived and allowed, in earlier times, to continue as a breed. Incidentally, in 1873 Stonehenge mentions in *On The Dog*, that all varieties of Spaniels were expected to give tongue on scent and that the owner of a

Ch. Easdale's Winsome Laddy a top winning parti-color of an earlier day.

truly valuable Spaniel could tell the kind of game it was running by the sound of the dog's voice. Today, of course, the Spaniel is severely penalized if it "sounds off" at all on game.

A few very abortive attempts to revive Cockers as sporting dogs were made in the early Twentieth Century, but died of their own inertia. Here and there sporting gentlemen used Cockers and boasted of the "birdiness" of their dogs but, for the most part, there was little or no interest in the Cocker as a gun dog.

Then type began to change in the breed. The long, low-slung, useless type was passing and a short-backed, square and cobby dog that could move and had stamina and endurance was taking its place. The Cocker was assuming the shape, the outline, the body and vigor of a sporting dog again. Then in 1923, a change came in the Cocker's future, due initially to the efforts of Mrs. Ella B. Moffit, and ably aided by Freeman Lloyd, then kennel editor of

*By Midkiff Miracle Man and out of Sand Spring
Pixie, The good bitch, Ch. Pleasant Hill Sue,
was bred by W. G. Hark.*

*Overcross Eros, a champion stud owned and bred
by Mrs. Haley Fiske, was sired by Walls
Bob-O-Link x Overcross Iris.*

*A fine son of Red Brucie, Ch. Windsweep
Ladysman (1932) was bred and owned by
Miss Alice Dodsworth. His dam was Cordova Clare.*

*Prince Tom III, the famous little Cocker owned by
Tom Clute who, though bred from pet stock,
became a top dog in obedience (U.D.) and a
field trial champion.*

Field & Stream magazine, and subsequently helped by Elias Vail, Clarence Pfaffenberger, Frank Dole, Dr. Bruette and Ralph Craig and, last but not least, Mrs. Moffit's show champion Rowcliffe Red Man. Sired by Red Brucie and bred by Mr. Mellenthin, this grand little dog, from show stock, had nevertheless inherited a vast amount of natural hunting instinct from earlier ancestors, and showed, with gay integrity, what a Cocker could do in the field. The efforts of this fine group brought the Cocker back from oblivion as a sporting dog and gave to him again his rightful heritage in the hunting field.

In 1924 field trials for Cockers were initiated in America and one of the first greats, appropriately enough, came from Mrs. Moffit's kennels, Rowcliffe War Dance. This admirable little Spaniel showed the American sporting world that a good Cocker was capable of defeating even the best of Springers in the field.

There have been many great sporting Cockers since that time, true working Cockers of the caliber of the brilliant Field Trial Champion Blue Waters Magnificent, the Dual Champion My Own High Time, Rowcliffe Sensation and High Time Sensation among others. One of the most recent is Prince Tom III, owned by Tom Clute of Michigan, who won just about everything a Cocker can win in the field and did it the hard way. Prince was from pet stock and, besides winning international fame in field Trials, was also an International Champion in Obedience trials. This great little Cocker did the breed a tremendous service for good through exposure on TV, personal appearances, and through the book that tells his whimsical and heart-warming story. The book has become a children's classic of its kind. I had the pleasure of illustrating it and used Prince Tom himself as a model. This little Cocker is truly an unusual dog, one of the most intelligent dogs of any breed that I have ever known.

The American Cocker's place in the sporting scene is now firmly established and his worth as a hunting companion can no longer be denied.

Owned, handled and bred by Mrs. Harry Reno,
of Port Huron, Michigan, this photo shows
American and Canadian Ch. Abbis Mister A.O.K.
winning the group at the Canadian National
Sportsmen's Show in 1965.

III

Inheritance in the Cocker Spaniel

DARWIN'S THEORY

Down through the ages, from the time that early man first became aware of himself as an entity and probed questioningly at the world around him, men of splendid and inquiring minds bent their efforts to shed light upon the mystery of specie origin. It remained for one man to find the key to the origin of species; that man was, of course, Charles Robert Darwin. He found the answer to the puzzle of life in evolution, the theory that all life-forms find kinship through a common and basic ancestry and that divergence occurs to permit variety to fit possible changes in environment.

Due to Darwin's principles, science knew that natural selection produced changes in all living things. But how? There seemed to be no rules that could be followed to an end result. There had to be a pattern of inheritance, but what was it and how did it work?

Darwin had asked these questions, too, as did the men of science who came after him. But he, like them, could find no definite answer. Darwin did not know that his basic laws of evolution and the fundamental rules of heredity were being developed at approximately the same time. But Darwin's great book, *The Origin of Species*, in which his evolutionary (and revolutionary) theory was advanced, was published in 1859. It was not until 1900, however, that the laws governing inheritable linkage were made known to the world.

In the interim, superstition, arrogant and baseless theorizing, took the place of truth in advancing so-called formulas of inheritance. The inheritance of acquired characteristics is one of the fallacious theories that was widely believed and has its disciples even today. Birthmarking is another false theory which must be discarded in the light of present-day genetical knowledge. The genes which give our dogs all their inheritable material are isolated in the body from any environmental influence. What the host does or has done to him influences them not at all. The so-called "proofs" advanced by the adherents of both these bogus theories were simply isolated coincidences.

Telegony is another of the untrue beliefs about influencing inherited characteristics. This is the theory that the sire of one litter could or would influence the progeny of a future litter out of the same bitch but sired by an entirely different stud. Telegony is, in its essence, comparable to the theory of saturation—which is the belief that if a bitch is bred many times in succession to the same stud, she will become so "saturated" with his "blood "that she will produce only puppies of his type, even when mated to an entirely different stud. By far the strongest and most widely believed was the theory that the blood was the vehicle through which all inheritable material was passed from parents to offspring, from one generation to the next. The taint of that superstition still persists in the phraseology we employ in our breeding terms such as "bloodlines," "percentage of blood," "pure-blooded," "blue-blooded," etc. This "blood" reference in regard to heredity crops up in all places and for all allied references, as witness the politician who cries vehemently, "I am proud that the blood of Paul Revere runs in my veins!" To achieve such a remarkable accomplishment would require transfusion from a long-dead corpse.

THE DISCOVERY OF GENETICS

The truth was found in spite of such a persistent theory, and in the history of science there is no more dramatic story than that of the discovery of the true method of inheritance. No, the truth was not arrived at in some fine endowed scientific laboratory gleaming with the mysterious implements of research. The scene was instead a small dirt garden in Moravia, which is now a part of Czechoslovakia. Here Johann Gregor Mendel, a Moravian monk, planted and crossed several varieties of common garden peas and quietly recorded the differences that occurred through several generations. Over a period of eight years this remarkable man continued his studies. Then, in 1865, he read a paper he had prepared regarding his experiments to the local Brunn, a society of historians and naturalists. The society subsequently published this paper in its journal, which was obscure and definitely limited in distribution.

Now we come to the amazing part of this story, for Mendel's theory of inheritance, which contained the fundamental laws upon which all modern advances in genetics have been based, gathered dust for thirty-four years, and it seemed that one of the most important scientific discoveries of the nineteenth century was to be lost to mankind. Then in 1900, sixteen years after Mendel's death, the paper was rediscovered and his great work given to the world.

34

In his experiments with the breeding of garden peas, Mendel discovered and identified the units of heredity. He found that when two individual plants which differed in a unit trait were mated, one trait appeared in the offspring, and one did not. The trait which was visible he named the "dominant" trait, and the one which was not visible he called the "recessive" trait. He proposed that traits, such as color, are transmitted by means of units in the sex cells and that one of these units must be pure, let us say either black or white, but never be a mixture of both. From a black parent which is pure for that trait, only black units are transmitted, and from a white parent, only white units can be passed down. But when one parent is black and one is white, a hybrid occurs which transmits both the black and white units in equal amounts. The hybrid itself will take the color of the dominant parent, yet carry the other color as a recessive. Various combinations of unit crosses were tried by Mendel, and he found that there were six possible ways in which a pair of determiners (Mendel's "units") could combine with a similar pair. The Mendelian chart shows how this law of Mendel's operates and the expected results. This simple Mendelian law holds true in the actual breeding of all living things—of plants, mice, humans, or Cocker Spaniels.

HOW HEREDITY WORKS

The beginning of new life in animals arises from the union of a male sperm and a female egg cell during the process of breeding. Each sperm cell has a nucleus containing one set of chromosomes, which are small packages, or units, of inheritable material. Each egg also possesses a nucleus of one set of chromosomes. The new life formed by the union of sperm cell and egg cell

then possesses two sets of chromosomes—one from the sperm, one from the egg, or one set from the sire and one set from the dam. For when the sperm cell enters the egg, it does two things—it starts the egg developing and it adds a set of chromosomes to the set already in the egg. Here is the secret of heredity. For in the chromosomes lie the living genes that shape the destiny of the unborn young. Thus we see that the pattern of heredity, physical and mental, is transmitted to our dog from its sire and dam through tiny living cells called genes, which are the connecting links between the puppy and his ancestors.

These packets of genes, the chromosomes, resemble long, paired strings of beads. Each pair is alike, the partners formed the same, yet differing from the like partners of the next pair. In the male we find the exception to this rule, for here there is one pair of chromosomes composed of two that are not alike. These are the sex chromosomes, and in the male they are different from those in the female in that the female possesses a like pair while the male does not. If we designate the female chromosomes as X, then the female pair is XX. The male too has an X chromosome, but its partner is a Y chromosome. If the male X chromosome unites with the female X chromosome, then the resulting embryo will be a female. But if the male Y chromosome is carried by the particular sperm that fertilizes the female egg, the resulting progeny will be a male. It is, therefore, a matter of chance as to what sex the offspring will be, since the sperm is capricious and fertilization is random.

The actual embryonic growth of the puppy is a process of division of cells to form more and more new cells and at each cell division of the fertilized egg each of the two sets of chromosomes provided by sire and dam also divide, until all the myriad divisions of cells and chromosomes have reached an amount necessary to form a complete and living entity. Then birth becomes an accomplished fact, and we see before us a living, squealing puppy.

What is he like, this puppy? He is what his controlling genes have made him. His sire and dam have contributed one gene of each kind to their puppy, and this gene which they have given him is but one of the two which each parent possesses for a particular characteristic. Since he has drawn these determiners at random they can be either dominant or recessive genes. His dominant heritage we can see when he develops, but what he possesses in recessive traits is hidden.

There are rules governing dominant and recessive traits useful in summarizing what is known of the subject at the present time. We can be reasonably sure that a dominant trait: (1) Does not skip a generation. (2) Will affect a relatively large number of the progeny. (3) Will be carried only by the affected individuals. (4) Will minimize the danger of continuing undesirable characteristics in a strain. (5) Will make the breeding formula of each individual quite certain.

With recessive traits we note that: (1) The trait may skip one or more generations. (2) On the average a relatively small percentage of the individuals in the strain carry the trait. (3) Only those individuals which carry a pair of determiners for the trait, exhibit it. (4) Individuals carrying only one determiner can be ascertained only by mating. (5) The trait must come through both sire and dam.

MENDELIAN EXPECTATION CHART

The six possible ways in which a pair of detirminers can unite. Ratios apply to expectancy over large numbers, except in lines no. 1, 2, and 6, where exact expectancy is realized in every litter.

| PROGENY | SIRE AND DAM |

You will hear some breeders say that the bitch contributes 60 per cent or more to the excellence of the puppies. Others swear that the influence of the sire is greater than that of the dam. Actually, the puppy receives 50 per cent of his germ plasm from each, though one parent may be so dominant that it seems that the puppy received most of his inheritable material from that parent. From the fact that the puppy's parents also both received but one set of determiners from each of their parents and in turn have passed on but one of their sets to the puppy, it would seem that one of those sets that the grandparents contributed has been lost and that therefore the puppy has inherited the germ plasm from only two of its grandparents, not four. But selection is random, and it is possible for the puppy's four grandparents to contribute an equal 25 per cent of all the genes inherited, or various and individual percentages, one grandparent contributing more and another less. It is even possible for the pup to inherit no genes at all from one grandparent and 50 per cent from another.

Chromosomes in
nucleus of cell.

Chromosomes arranged in
pairs, showing partnership.

The genes that have fashioned this puppy of ours are of chemical composition and are living cells securely isolated from any outside influence, a point which we have made before and which bears repeating. Only certain kinds of man-directed radiation, some poisons or other unnatural means can cause change in the genes. No natural means can influence them. Environment can effect an individual but not his germ plasm. For instance, if the puppy's nutritional needs are not fully provided for during his period of growth, his end potential will not be attained; but regardless of his outward appearance, his germ plasm remains inviolate and capable of passing on to the next generation the potential that was denied him by improper feeding.

Breeding fine Cockers would be a simple procedure if all characteristics were governed by simple Mendelian factors, but alas, this is not so. Single genes are not solely responsible for single characteristics, mental or physical. The complexity of any part of the body and its dependence upon other parts in order to function properly makes it obvious that we must deal with interlocking blocks of controlling genes in a life pattern of chain reaction.

Ch. Rowcliffe Confidence, bred by Ralph C. Craig,
owned by Mrs. Frank Sterns.
sire: Rowcliffe Vagabond dam: Craigden's Comely

Ch. Sand Spring Superman, 1924,
bred by W. T. Payne.
sire: Midkiff Miracle Man   dam: Midkiff Jean

Eye color, for instance, is determined by a simple genetic factor, but the ability to see, the complicated mechanism of the eye, the nerves, the blood supply, the retina and iris, even how your Cocker reacts to what he sees, are all part of the genetic pattern of which eye color is but a segment.

Since they are living cells in themselves, the genes can and do change, or mutate. In fact, it is thought now that many more gene mutations take place than were formerly suspected, but that the great majority are either within the animal, where they cannot be seen, or are so small in general scope that they are overlooked. The dramatic mutations which affect the surface are the ones we notice and select for or against according to whether they direct us toward our goal or away from it. Again, with the vagary inherent in all living things, the mutated gene can change once again back to its original form.

This etching by Bert Cobb is a fine study of heads of top Rowcliffe Cockers. Here are Ch. Vagabond, out of Tokalon Cookie, Ch. Ringleader, sire of Vagabond, by Rowcliffe Le Noir x Rowcliffe Princess, and Sally, by Midkiff Creme de la Creme x Cricket VI. All these dogs were whelped in the 1920's.

We see then that the puppy is the product of his germ plasm, which has been handed down from generation to generation. We know that there are certain rules that generally govern the pattern that the genes form and that a gene which prevents another gene from showing in an individual is said to be a dominant and the repressed gene a recessive. Remember, the animal itself is not dominant or recessive in color or any other characteristic. It is the gene that is dominant or recessive, as judged by results. We find that an animal can contain in each of his body cells a dominant and a recessive gene. When this occurs, the dog is said to be heterozygous. As illustrated in the chart we know that there is an opposite to the heterozygous individual, an animal which contains two genes of the same kind in its cells—either two dominants or two recessives—and this animal is said to be homozygous. The loss of a gene or the gain of a gene, or the process of change among the genes, is known as mutation, and the animal affected is called a mutant.

Every bitch that stands before us, every stud we intend to use, is not just one dog, but two. Every living thing is a Jekyll and Hyde, shadow and substance. The substance is the Cocker that lives and breathes and moves before us, the animal that we see, the physical manifestation of the interaction of genotypic characters and environment—the "phenotype." The shadow is the Cocker we don't see, yet this shadow is as much a part of the dog before us as the animal we see. This shadow-Cocker is the gene-complex, or total collection of its genes—the "genotype." The visual substance is easily evaluated, but the invisible shadow must also be clearly seen and evaluated, for both shadow and substance equally contribute to the generations to come. Without understanding the complete genetic picture of any particular dog, we cannot hope to successfully use that dog to accomplish specific results. In order to understand, we must delve into the genetic background of the animal's ancestry until the shadow becomes as clearly discernible as the substance and we can evaluate the dog's genetic worth as a whole; for this dog that stands before us is but the containing vessel, the custodian of a specific pattern of heredity.

INHERITED MENTAL CHARACTERISTICS

Mental aptitudes in the Cocker's pattern of heredity follow the same genetic paths as does its physical makeup. The early Spaniels used in the field all gave tongue when the quarry was scented. This was desirable in those days when the Spaniel was used in falconry or to start game for the coursing hounds. But in our modern Cocker gun dog it is an unwanted characteristic. Through rigid selection for silent trailers the trait was "fixed" in the breed. Since experiments in this area indicate that open trailing, or giving tongue on scent, is a dominant characteristic and "still" trailing a recessive, it follows that to establish the wanted still trailing ability it was necessary to select for recessives and establish these recessives in the breed in a "pure" state.

Hunting with the nose to the ground is another characteristic of the Spaniel family (as it is of the hound family) that has been "fixed," or firmly established genetically, by rigid selection. Cockers are also natural tree dogs and can do as fine a job of treeing game as any hound bred specifically for the purpose. The ability to retrieve is also an inherited factor that varies in intensity with the hereditary pattern of the individual dog.

It is amazing how mental aptitudes will persist in a breed even through many generations in which selection for these characteristics has not been made. A case in point in the Cocker breed is the famous field trial winner Prince Tom III. Prince is the result of generations of ordinary pet-stock breeding, yet in him all the instinctive hunting ability of long-ago ancestors fortuitiously blended in his germ plasm to produce a dog of tremendous excellence in the field. In this case the innate gundog abilities of Prince Tom were aided by an almost uncanny canine intelligence

GENETIC INFLUENCE ON COAT AND COLOR

Genetic studies of coat quality and color in the Cocker Spaniel indicate that thin coats are dominant over heavy coats. A heavy coated dog, therefore, is the result of paired recessives and when bred to another heavy coated animal of the opposite sex will produce heavy coated progeny. The colors white and red seem to carry a length inhibiting factor, while black will give the dog the maximum length of hair possible for its specific strain. By studying parti-colored coats, black and white and red and white, the difference in hair length can be easily seen. Coarseness of hair is also dominant over the finer type of coat.

The mode of inheritance in coat color of the Cocker Spaniel follows closely the same genetic pattern as most other breeds of dogs where a variety of coat colors is permissible.

Solid colors are dominant over the white spotting of parti-colors. Black and white partis will exhibit greater areas of pigmentation than will red and white parti-colored dogs. Black is dominant over all other Cocker colors. Liver is essentially black with a genetic factor that inhibits the black pigment. Liver, therefore behaves like black but is recessive to a double dominant black. Liver colored noses, foot pads, lips and eyelids and comparatively light eyes are inherited factors that are characteristic of this inhibited color.

A black saddle factor that is a genetic characteristic of some red colored families acts as a modifier of the solid red color to produce the black-and-tan variety. This combination color can come from reds or blacks that carry red as a recessive as well as from black-and-tans. When coupled with the white spotting piebald or parti factor the result is a tricolor. Liver-and-tan follows the same pattern of inheritance as black-and-tan but is recessive to it. Pure black-nosed reds are recessive to black and, since liver is a modified black, when liver and black-nosed red are bred together the resulting progeny are black.

Dilute or pastel colors are recessive to pure colors. In the red color series there are a number of dilute shades, from deep gold to pale cream. Blue is not seen too frequently in Cockers but, when it does appear, it is recognized as a dilute influence in the black series.

In parti-colored dogs breeders can, by selection, produce almost exactly the ratio of white and color that they desire and, genetically, even paint the

Ch. My Own Hope, by the great Red Brucie x My Own Lady, bred by Herman E. Mellinthin (of course) and owned by Windsweep Kennels. A lovely portrait shot of a lovely dog.

Below is Ch. The Great My Own, a grandson of Red Brucie through his sire, My Own Peter Manning. The dam was My Own Vixen.

color where they want it. Alas, like most happy theories that work, other factors rear their ugly heads and parti-color breeders will tell you that the pups who carry the markings they have been striving for are generally not the best pups in the litter. So, by too strict selection for parti-color perfection in markings, the stock can become down-graded in type and defeat the whole purpose of the breeding program.

The factor that produces roan (seen more frequently in English Cockers) is dominant over the ticking factor, and the latter is dominant over white. Blue roan (since the basis is black) is dominant over strawberry roan (red basis).

Remember that if you use a solid colored dog to bring improvement to a parti-colored strain that the solid color can mask parti-colored recessive genes of an undesirable pattern.

White Cockers with dark noses, eyes, foot-pads and eyelids are seen occasionally. They are quite often basically reds of light pigmentation upon which a dilution factor has been at work. There is, though, a dark-eyed white that is pure and is not of the red family. Albino whites, sporting the characteristic "pink" eyes, are not recommended for breeding and are seldom seen as most breeders recognize albinism and eliminate these puppies in the nest. All of these whites are recessive to all other Cocker colors.

MODERN GENETIC DISCOVERIES

With the basic concept of heredity that Mendel found as a foundation other scientists went forward to fantastic new discoveries in this new and fertile scientific field. The units of inheritance, the genes, were studied and their behavior catalogued. Finally it was found that there was a chemical powder, DNA (deoxyribonucleic acid), and another, similar nucleic acid called RNA (ribonucleic acid) in chromosomes that were, with protein, the materials of heredity.

DNA has complete domination over all cells and is able to constantly reproduce itself. So indescribably minute that it requires an enormous electronic microscope to become visible, it is yet so omniscient that it contains within itself a creative diversity to command uncountable billions of forms. This remarkable chemical is composed of four nucleotides which produce twenty universal amino acids which, in turn, produce over 100,000 proteins that give shape, form and substance to the infinite diversity of life-forms on this earth.

The study of genetics continues as men delve deeper into cause and effect, What we know today of inheritance is of immeasurable importance in animal breeding, removing a great deal of the guesswork from our operations. Yet we do not know enough to make the breeding of top stock a cut-and-dried

Ch. Windridge Bell of Washington

Ch. Claythorne Courageous

matter, or to reduce it to the realm of pure science, with a definite answer to every problem. Perhaps this is where the fascination lies. Life is spontaneous and many times unstable, so that even with the greater knowledge that the future will no doubt bring, it is possible that the breeding of top animals will still remain a combination of science and art, with a touch of necessary genius and aesthetic innovation, to ever lend fascination to this riddle of inheritance. *

---

* For more comprehensive information on the art of breeding, see the author's book, DOG BREEDERS' HANDBOOK.

Ch. My-Ida-Ho Squareshooter.
sire: Ch. Stonewalk Squareshooter
dam: My-Ida-Ho All Smiles
Owned by Maurice and Joan Ferrero and bred by
My-Ida-Ho Kennels, Squareshooter, handled by
John Davidson, is shown going Best Of Variety,
from the classes over specials, under judge
Herman Cox at the Oakland Kennel Club.

IV

Basic Breeding Techniques

In today's mechanistic world, with its rushing pace and easy pleasures, much of the creative urge in man has been throttled. We who breed dogs are extremely fortunate, for in our work we have a real creative outlet—we are in the position of being able to mold beauty and utility in living flesh and blood. Our tools are the genes of inheritance, and our art, their infinite combination. We have the power to create a work of living art that will show the evidence of our touch for generations to come.

Now that we have absorbed some of the basic facts of heredity, we can, with greater understanding, examine the various kinds of breeding which can be used in perpetuating wanted characteristics. We have learned that within the design of the germ plasm great variation occurs. But within the breed itself as a whole, we have an average, or norm, which the great majority of Cockers mirror. Draw a straight horizontal line on a piece of paper and label this line, "norm." Above this line draw another and label it, "above norm." This latter line represents the top dogs, the great ones, and the length of this line will be very much shorter than the length of the "norm" line. Below the "norm" line draw still another line, designating this to be, "below norm." These are the animals possessing faults which we do not wish to perpetuate.

Since the time of the first registered Cocker the number of breeders who have molded the characteristics of the breed have been legion. So many have bred without a basic knowledge of any of the fundamentals that the stock produced has the detrimental effect of dangerously lowering the norm. Examine the pedigrees of your dogs, and in many instances you will find an example of this—a line incorporated in your pedigree that causes worry to the true student of breeding. The real objective of all breeding is to raise

47

Two beautiful black and white partis. Ch. Begays Yes Indeedy, sired by Ch. Twinhavens Casey x Merrikays War Bonnet, winning parti at the 1966 A.S.C. Futurity. At the right is Ch. Begays Bangalore, the youngest bitch to ever win at the American Spaniel Club show. Both these Cockers are owned and were bred by Bill Ernst.

49

the norm of a given breed and thereby approach always closer to the breed standard.

If we are to achieve the greatest good from any program of breeding, there are four important traits which we must examine. It is essential that these traits should never depart from the norm.

The first is fertility. The lack of this essential in any degree must be guarded against diligently.

The second is vigor. Loss of vigor, or hardiness, and its allied ills, such as lowered resistance to disease, finicky eating, etc., will lead to disaster.

Longevity is the third important trait. An individual of great worth—who represents a fortunate combination of excellent characteristics which he dominantly passes on to his offspring—must be useful for a long time after his or her worth is recognized by the progeny produced.

The fourth is temperament. Here is the sum total of the dog's usefulness to man in the various categories in which he serves. Lack of true Cocker character nullifies any other advances which you may make in your breeding program.

The norm can be likened to the force of gravity, possessing a powerful pull toward itself, so that regression toward the average is strong, even though you have used in your breeding parents which are both above average. The same holds true for progeny bred from animals below norm, but from these you will get a lesser number which reach the mean average and a greater number which remain below norm. In the case of the better-than-average parents, some of the progeny will stay above the norm line and the majority will regress. Occasionally a dog of superior structure is produced by a poor family, but inevitably this animal is useless as a stud because he will produce all his objectionable family traits and none of the fortuitous characteristics he displays in himself. From a breeding standpoint it is far better to use an average individual from top stock than a top individual from average or below-average stock. It is also true that many times a great show dog produces average progeny while his little-known brother, obscured by the shadow of the great dog's eminence, produces many above-average young. This is not as strange as it sounds when we consider the fact that the individual animal is the custodian of his germ plasm and it is this germ plasm that produces, not the individual. In this instance, due to variation in the germ plasm, the top dog does not possess the happy genetic combinations that his average brother does and so cannot produce stock of comparative value.

Any of the various categories of breeding practice which we will outline can be followed for the betterment of the breed if used intelligently. Regardless of which practice one follows, there generally comes a time when it is necessary to incorporate one or more of the other forms into the breeding

Ch. Bubble Up of Stockdale.
sire: Sand Spring Follow Through
dam: Dinah of Stockdale
Whelped in 1931. Owned and bred by C. B. Van
Meter.

Below: Ch. Stockdale Town Talk.
Beautiful type and balance, from the same kennel
as Bubble Up.

program in order to concentrate certain genetic characters, or to introduce new ones which are imperative for over-all balance. Outcross breeding is not recommended as a consistent practice. Rather, it is a valuable adjunct to the other methods when used as a corrective measure.

INBREEDING

By breeding father to daughter, half brother to half sister, son to mother, and, by closest inbreeding of all, brother to sister, stability and purity of inherited material is obtained. Specifically, inbreeding concentrates both good features and faults, strengthening dominants and bringing recessives out into the open where they can be seen and evaluated. It supplies the breeder with the only control he can have over prepotency and homozygosity, or the combining and balancing of similar genetic factors. Inbreeding does not produce degeneration, it merely concentrates weaknesses already present so that they can be recognized and eliminated. This applies to both physical and psychical hereditary transmission.

Ch. Country Gossip. Nice coat, good balance and well bred, this Cocker did some nice winning in top competition.

The most important phases of inbreeding are: (1) To choose as nearly faultless partners as is possible; (2) To cull, or select, rigidly from the resultant progeny.

Selection is always important regardless of which breeding procedure is used, but in inbreeding it becomes imperative. It is of interest to note that the most successful inbreeding programs have used as a base an animal which was either inbred or line-bred. To the breeder, the inbred animal represents an individual whose breeding formula has been so simplified that certain results can almost always be depended upon.

There are many examples of extreme inbreeding over a period of generations in other animal and plant life. Perhaps the most widely known are the experimental rats bred by Dr. Helen L. King, which are the result of over one hundred generations of direct brother and sister mating. The end result has been bigger, finer rodents than the original pair, and entirely dependable uniformity. Dr. Leon F. Whitney has bred and developed a beautiful strain

*Ch. Elenita of California was whelped in 1927
in the kennels of Mrs. R. A. Schroeder.
She was by Knebworth Cyclone x Werita.*

*Ch. Sand Spring Follow Through below, whelped
in 1929, was a well known and liked Cocker in
his day. Bred by Mrs. L'Hommedieu he was one
(though a top one) of the famous Sand Spring
string of Cockers.
sire: Sand Spring Surmise
dam: Sand Spring Smiling Through.*

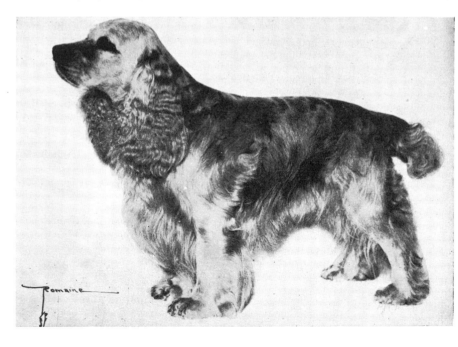

of tropical fish, *Lebistes reticulatis*, commonly known as "guppies," by consecutive brother to sister breeding for ten generations. Dr. Whitney found that each succeeding generation was a little smaller and less vigorous, but that in the fifth generation a change occurred for the better, and in each generation thereafter, size, vigor, and color improved. This pattern should hold true with all life forms developed from the same type of breeding.

It is interesting to note that genetic experiments with plants, vegetables, and animals which we consider lower in the evolutionary scale than our beloved dogs have shown that when two intensely inbred lines of consecutive brother and sister matings are crossed, the resultant progeny are larger than the original heterozygous stock and possess hybrid vigor such as the mongrel possesses, which enables him to exist even under environmental neglect (heterosis).

Can dog breeders indulge in such concentrated inbreeding with stock, as has been attempted successfully by scientists with other genetic material? We don't know, simply because, to my knowledge, it has never been tried. It would be an expensive undertaking to keep two or more lines progressing of direct brother and sister inbreedings; to cull and destroy, always keeping the best pair as breeding partners for the next generation. Lethal faults, hitherto unsuspected in the stock, might become so drastically concentrated as to bring the experiment to a premature conclusion, even if one had the time, money, and energy to attempt it. But such is the inherent character of germ plasm that one direct outcross will bring complete normality to an inbred line drastically weakened by its own concentrated faults.

It is essential that the breeder have a complete understanding of the merits of inbreeding, for by employing it skillfully results can be obtained to equal those found in other animal-breeding fields. We must remember that inbreeding in itself creates neither faults nor virtues, it merely strengthens and fixes them in the resulting animals. If the basic stock used is generally good, possessing but few, and those minor, faults, then inbreeding will concentrate all those virtues which are so valuable in that basic stock. Inbreeding gives us great breeding worth by its unique ability to produce prepotency and unusual similarity of type. It exposes the "skeletons in the closet" by bringing to light hitherto hidden faults, so that they may be selected against. We do not correct faults by inbreeding, therefore, we merely make them recognizable so they can be eliminated. The end result of inbreeding, coupled with rigid selection, is complete stability of the breeding material.

With certain strains inbreeding can be capricious, revealing organic weaknesses never suspected that result in decreased vitality, abnormalities—physical and mental—or lethal or crippling factors. Unfortunately, it is not possible to foretell results when embarking on such a program, even if seemingly robust and healthy breeding partners are used as a base. The best chance of success generally comes from the employment of animals which themselves have been strongly inbred and have not been appreciably weakened by it in any way.

An interesting development frequently found in inbreeding is in the extremes produced. The average progeny from inbreeding is equal to the average from line-breeding or outbreeding, but the extremes are greater than those produced by either of the latter breeding methods. Inbreeding, then, is at once capable of producing the best and the worst, and these degrees can be found present in the same litter.

Here again, in inbreeding, as in most of the elements of animal husbandry, we must avoid thinking in terms of human equations. Whether for good or ill, your Cocker was man-made, and his destiny and that of his progeny lie in your hands. By selection you improve the strain, culling and killing misfits and monsters. Mankind indulges in no such practice of purification of the race. He mates without any great mental calculation or plan for the future generation. His choice of a mate is both geographically and socially limited in scope. No one plans this mating of his for the future betterment of the breed. Instead, he is blindly led by emotions labeled "love," and sometimes by lesser romantics, "desire." For our Cockers we want something vastly better than the hit-and-miss proposition that has been the racial procedure of man.

Another type of inbreeding, which is not practiced as much as it should be, is "backcrossing." Here we think largely in terms of the male dog, since the element of time is involved. The process involves finding a superior breeding male who is so magnificent in type that we want to perpetuate his qualities and produce, as closely as we can, the prototype of this certain individual. This good male is bred to a fine bitch, and the best female pup who is similar to her sire in type is bred back again to her sire. Again, the best female pup is selected and bred back to her sire. This is continued as long as the male can reproduce, or until weaknesses become apparent (if they do) that make it impractical to continue. If this excellent male seems to have acquired his superiority through the genetic influence of his mother, the first breeding made should possibly be the mating of son to mother, and the subsequent breeding as described above. In each litter the bitch retained to backcross to her sire should, of course, greatly mirror the sire's type.

LINE-BREEDING

Line-breeding is a broader kind of inbreeding that conserves valuable characteristics by concentration and in a general sense gives us some control of type but a lesser control over specific characteristics. It creates "strains,"

A fine head study of a well
known Cocker of yesteryear,
Ch. Sugartown Pie.

Below
is Ch. Craigden Comely,
owned by the Sirdar
Kennels in Canada.
sire: Lucknow Creme de la
Creme
dam: Craigden First Lady
(a Red Brucie daughter).

or "families," within the breed which are easily recognized by their similar conformation. This is the breeding method used by most of the larger kennels, with varied success, since it is not extreme and therefore relatively safe. It is also the method the neophyte is generally advised to employ, for the same reasons.

Specifically, line-breeding entails the selection of breeding partners who have, in their pedigrees, one or more common ancestors. These individuals (or individual) occur repeatedly within the first four or five generations, so that it can be assumed their genetic influence molds the type of succeeding generations. It is a fact that in many breeds success has been obtained by line-breeding to outstanding individuals.

The method varies greatly in intensity, so that some dogs may be strongly line-bred, while others only remotely so. Selection is an important factor here, too, for if we line-breed to procure the specific type of a certain fine animal, then we must select in succeeding generations breeding stock which is the prototype of that individual, or our reason for line-breeding is lost.

One of the chief dangers of line-breeding can be contributed by the breeder of the strain. Many times the breeder reaches a point where he selects his breeding partners on pedigree alone, instead of by individual selection and pedigree combined, within the line.

In some instances intense line-breeding, particularly when the individual line-bred is to known to be prepotent, can have all the strength of direct inbreeding.

To found a strain which has definite characteristics, within the breed, the following recommendations, based mainly on the work of Humphrey and Warner and Kelley and Whitney, can be used as a guide.

1. Decide what few traits are essential and what faults are intolerable. Vigor, fertility, character, and temperament must be included in these essentials.

2. Develop a scoring system and score selected virtues and faults in accordance with your breeding aim. Particular stress should be put upon scoring for individual traits which need improvement.

3. Line-breed consistently to the best individuals produced which, by the progeny test, show that they will further improve the strain. Inbreeding can be indulged in if the animal used is of exceptional quality and with no outstanding faults. Outcrossings can be made to bring in wanted characteristics if they are missing from the basic stock. Relationship need not be close in the foundation animals, since wide outcrosses will give greater variation and therefore offer a much wider selection of desirable trait combinations.

Every Cocker used in this breeding program to establish a strain must be rigidly assessed for individual and breeding excellence and the average excellence of its relatives and its progeny.

OUTCROSS BREEDING

Outcross breeding is the choosing of breeding partners whose pedigrees, in the first five or six generations, are free from any common ancestry. With our Cockers we cannot outcross in the true sense of the term, since the genetic basis of all Cockers is built upon the germ plasm of a few selected individuals. To outcross completely, using the term literally (complete heterozygosity), it would be necessary to use an individual of an alien breed as one of the breeding partners.

For the breeder to exercise any control over the progeny of an outcross mating, one of the partners should be inbred or closely line-bred. The other partner should show, in himself and by the progeny test when bred to other bitches, that he is dominant in the needed compensations which are the reasons for the outcross. Thus, by outcross breeding, we bring new and needed characteristics into a strain, along with greater vigor and, generally, a lack of uniformity in the young. Greater uniformity can be achieved if the outcross is made between animals of similar family type. Here again we have a breeding method which has produced excellent individuals, since it tends to conceal recessive genes and promote individual merit. But it generally leads to a lower breeding worth in the outbred animal by dispersing favorable genetic combinations which have given us strain uniformity.

Outcross breeding can be likened to a jigsaw puzzle. We have a puzzle made up of pieces of various shapes and sizes which, when fitted together form a certain pattern. This basic puzzle is comparable to our line-bred or inbred strain. But in this puzzle there are a few pieces that we would like to change, and in so doing change the finished puzzle pattern for the better. We outcross by removing some of the pieces and reshaping them to our fancy, remembering that these new shapes also affect the shapes of the adjoining pieces, which must then be slightly altered for perfect fit. When this has been successfully accomplished, the finished pattern has been altered to suit our pleasure—we hope.

It sometimes happens that a line-bred or inbred bitch will be outcross bred to a stud possessed of an open pedigree. It would be assumed by the breeder that the bitch's family type would dominate in the resulting progeny. But occasionally the stud proves himself to be strongly prepotent, and the young instead reflect his individual qualities, not those of the bitch. This can be good or bad, depending on what you are looking for in the resultant litter.

Incidently, when we speak of corrective, or compensation, breeding, we do not mean the breeding of extremes to achieve an intermediate effect. We

Ch. Alderbrook Tiger, a top-winning black and white Parti of some years ago.

Ch. Allview Chief Atahualpa, by Sand Spring Follow Through x Allview Adella.

At the bottom of the page is Ch. Idolita, owned by Mr. and Mrs. Strauss, sired by Black Nugget of Goldenstate x Dawn of Goldenstate.

would not breed an extremely shy bitch to an over aggressive or vicious stud in the hope of getting progeny of good temperament. The offspring of such a mating would show temperament faults of both the extremes. Neither would we breed a long legged bitch to a stud whose legs are too short. From such a breeding we could expect either long legs or short legs, but no intermediate possessing the desired leg length. Corrective, or compensation, breeding means the breeding of one partner which is lacking, or faulty, in any specific respect, to an animal which is normal or excellent in the particular area where the other partner is found lacking. In the resulting progeny we can expect to find some young which show the desired improvement.

To sum up briefly, we find that *inbreeding* brings us a fixity of type and simplifies the breeding formula. It strengthens desirable dominants and brings hidden and undesirable recessives to the surface where they can be recognized and possibly corrected by *outcross breeding*. When we have thus established definite improvement in type by rigid selection for wanted characteristics, we *line-breed* to create and establish a strain or family line which, in various degrees, incorporates and produces the improvements which have been attained.

In this maze of hidden and obvious genetic stirring, we must not forget the importance of the concrete essence that stands before us. The breeding partners must be examined as individuals in themselves, apart from the story their pedigrees tell us. For as individuals they have been fashioned by, and are the custodians of, their germ plasm, and mirror this fact in their being. Breedings made from paper study only are akin to human marriages arranged in youth by a third party without consulting the partners—they can be consummated but have small chance of success.

The importance of a pedigree lies in the knowledge we have of the individual animals involved. A fifteen-generation pedigree means nothing if we know nothing about the dogs mentioned. It is more important to extend your knowledge of three or four generations than to extend the pedigree itself. Of real guidance in breeding is a card-index system. This system should indicate clearly the faults and virtues of every pedigree name for at least three generations, with available information as to dominant and recessive traits and the quality of each animal's progeny. At the moment, such a system is practically impossible to achieve. There is little enough known, genetically, about living animals, and the virtues of dogs that are gone are distorted by time and sentiment.

The breeding of fine dogs is not a toy to be played with by children. For some of us it forms a nucleus of living, in the esthetic sense. We who give much of our time, thought, and energy to the production of superior stock are often disgusted and disillusioned by the breeding results of others who merely play at breeding. So often individuals long in the game advise the novice never to inbreed, but only to line-breed, since in this way the least harm can be done. There has been too much harm done already by novice breeders who should not have been encouraged to breed at all, except under the direct supervision or advice of an experienced or knowledgeable dog man. The people who compose what we term The Cocker Spaniel "fancy," belong to one of three categories: the novice, the amateur, and the professional. The novice is one who has recently become enamored of the breed, a tyro, a beginner. Many of them remain in that category indefinitely, due to lack of sincerity or reluctance to learn. Others, eager to absorb all they can, soon rise above the original status:

The professional is one who makes his livelihood from the dog game. His living or employment depends in whole or part upon his kennel activities. A professional must know his business well in order to make it a success, and the earnest professional generally does, though he may occasionally be guilty of breeding for the market.

Numerically, the largest category is that of the amateur. To these individuals the breeding, showing, hunting or training of Cockers is a serious hobby. Here are the students of the breed, the people who, in most instances, are well informed, yet avid for new knowledge that will aid in breed betterment.

Our novice is many times a charming person who loves his dogs passionately, provides them with more fancy vitamins and supplements than honest food, and treats them with a sloppy sentimentality that even a human baby would resent. He simply can't wait to breed his lovely bitch and have those adorable puppies. Of course he hasn't the time to acquire a bit of knowledge about the breed, or about the animals in his bitch's pedigree or the stud to which he is going to breed. How then will he have the time or knowledge to care for the pregnant bitch and the subsequent litter properly? Yet inevitably he does find time to listen to the pseudo-professional advice of several self-confessed authorities. In due time this novice is possessed of a litter of the cutest puppies you ever saw, which will in turn be sold to other novices (Heaven help them) as show and breeding prospects.

By far the greatest menace to the future of the breed is a particular type of wealthy novice. Possessed of the wherewithal to keep and breed any amount of dogs, and kennelmen to take care of them, this novice blunders arrogantly forward by virtue of the authority vested in him by his bankbooks and, unhampered by knowledge, breeds indiscriminately, producing litter upon litter of worthless stock. By the law of averages an occasional animal is produced that is fairly good. By cramming show classes with other of his mediocre stock and shipping, with professional handlers, to parts of the country where major wins can be made with fewer entries, he soon has champions which are extensively advertised at stud for other novices to breed to. In the end this novice generally, surprisingly and suddenly, blossoms out as a full blown "authority" and judge.

What has been written above is not to be construed as a sweeping condemnation of all novices. Without a constant influx of neophyte breeders, the breed would not be in the high place it is today. Many so-called novices bring to their new breed interest a vast store of canine knowledge collected by an inquiring mind and contact with other breeds.

To repeat, the novice is generally advised by the old-time breeder to begin his new hobby with a line-bred bitch, as this is the cautious approach which leaves the least margin for error. But what of that novice who is essentially what we call a born "dog man"? That individual who, for lack of better definition, we say has a "feel" for dogs, who seems to possess an added sense where dogs are concerned?

If this person has an inquiring mind, normal intelligence, and has been associated with other breeds, then the picture of him as the true novice changes. The old-timer will find many times that this "novice" frequently possesses information that the old-timer did not even know existed. This is especially true if the tyro has been exposed to some scientific learning in fields relative to animal advancement. Even experience, which is the old-timer's last-ditch stand, is negligible, for this knowledgeable "novice" can disregard the vagaries of experience with foreknowledge of expectancy.

In most instances this type of novice doesn't begin to think of breeding, or even owning a specimen of the breed, until he has made a thorough study of background, faults, virtues, and genetic characters. To him, imitation is not a prelude to success. Therefore the line-bred bitch, modeled by another's

Ch. Stockdale Startler

Ch. Eash's Golden Boy

ego, is not for him. The outcross bitch, whose genetic composition presents a challenge and which, by diligent study and application of acquired knowledge, can become the fountainhead of a strain of his own, is the answer to his need.

Some of what you have read here in reference to the novice may have seemed to be cruel caricature. Actually, it is not caricature, but it is cruel and is meant to stress a point. We realize that to some novices our deep absorption in all the many aspects of breed betterment may seem silly or ridiculous. But the genetic repercussion of breeding stupidity can echo down through generations, making a mockery of our own intense, sometimes heartbreaking, and often humble, striving toward an ideal.

V

Feeding

Your Cocker is a carnivore, a flesh eater. His teeth are not made for grinding as are human teeth, but are chiefly fashioned for tearing and severing. Over a period of years this fact has led to the erroneous conclusion that the dog must be fed mostly on muscle meat in order to prosper. Wolves, jackals, wild dogs, and foxes comprise the family Canidae to which your dog belongs. These wild relatives of the dog stalk and run down their living food in the same manner the dog would employ if he had not become attached to man. The main prey of these predators are the various hoofed herbivorous animals, small mammals and birds of their native habitat. The carnivores consume the entire body of their prey, not just the muscle meat alone. This manner of feeding has led some zoologists to consider the dog family as omnivorous (eater of both plant and animal matter), despite their obvious physical relationship to the carnivores.

You would assume, and rightly so, that the diet which keeps these wild cousins of the dog strong, healthy, and fertile could be depended upon to do the same for your Cocker. Of course, in this day and age your dog cannot live off the land. He depends upon you for sustenance, and to feed him properly, you must understand what essential food values the wild carnivore derives from his kill, for this is nature's supreme lesson in nutrition.

The canine hunter first laps the blood of his victim, then tears open the stomach and eats its contents, composed of predigested vegetable matter. He feasts on liver, heart, kidneys, lungs, and the fat-encrusted intestines. He

Ted Young, Jr. Handling the tri-color dog, Ch.
Meadow Lark Masquerade to Best of.Variety at the
Cocker Spaniel Club of Long Island Annual
Specialty. The dog is owned by Mrs. Phillip Smith,
and was given this nice win by judge
Mrs. Helen Considine.

crushes and consumes the bones and the marrow they contain, feeds on fatty meat and connective tissue, and finally eats the lean muscle meat. From the blood, bones, marrow, internal organs, and muscle meat he has absorbed minerals and proteins. The stomach and its contents have supplied vitamins and carbohydrates. From the intestines and fatty meat he gets fats, fatty acids, vitamins, and carbohydrates. Other proteins come from the ligaments and connective tissue. Hair and some indigestable parts of the intestinal contents provide enough roughage for proper laxation. From the sun he basks in and the water he drinks, he absorbs supplementary vitamins and minerals. From his kill, therefore, the carnivore acquires a well-rounded diet. To supply these same essentials to your Cocker in a form which you can easily purchase is the answer to his dietary needs.

BASIC FOODS AND SUPPLEMENTS

From the standpoint of nutrition, any substance may be considered food which can be used by an animal as a body-building material, a source of energy, or a regulator of body activity. From the preceding paragraphs we have learned that muscle meat alone will not fill these needs and that your Cocker's diet must be composed of many other food materials to provide elements necessary to his growth and health. These necessary ingredients can be found in any grocery store. There you can buy all the important natural sources of the dietary essentials listed below.

1. PROTEIN: meat, dairy products, eggs, soybeans.
2. FAT: butter, cream, oils, fatty meat, milk, cream cheese, suet.
3. CARBOHYDRATES: cereals, vegetables, confectionery syrups, honey.
4. VITAMIN A: greens, peas, beans, asparagus, broccoli, eggs, milk.
5. THIAMINE: vegetables, legumes, whole grains, eggs, muscle meats, organ meats, milk, yeast.
6. RIBOFLAVIN: green leaves, milk, *liver*, cottonseed flour or meal, egg yolk, wheat germ, yeast, beef, chicken.
7. NIACIN: milk, lean meats, liver, yeast.
8. VITAMIN D: fish that contains oil (salmon, sardine, herring, cod), fish liver oils, eggs, fortified milk.
9. ASCORBIC ACID: tomatoes, citrus fruits, raw cabbage (it has not been established that ascorbic acid is necessary for dogs).
10. IRON, CALCIUM, AND PHOSPHORUS: milk and milk products, vegetables, eggs, soybeans, bone marrow, blood, liver, oatmeal.

The first three listed essentials compliment each other and compose the basic nutritional needs. Proteins build new body tissue and are composed of amino acids, which differ in combination with the different proteins. Carbohydrates furnish the fuel for growth and energy, and fat produces heat

The results of good feeding are shown in your dog's coat, expression, and energy. To win in top competition like Ch. Nor-Mar's Nujac, shown below and owned by Marianne Doty, a Cocker must be fed correctly.

which becomes energy and enables the dog to store energy against emergency. Vitamins and minerals, in general, act as regulators of cell activity.

Proteins are essentially the basis of life, for living cells are composed of protein molecules. In this connection, an interesting scientific experiment was conducted a short while ago which led to an important discovery. A young scientist attempted to duplicate the conditions which, it is assumed, prevailed upon the earth before life began. Cosmological theory indicates that the atmosphere at that time (approximately two thousand million years ago, give or take a year) would have been poisonous to all the living organisms that exist today, with the exception of certain bacteria. When the experiment had been completed, it was found that amino acids had formed. These chemicals are the building blocks of proteins, and proteins are the basis of life. No, science has not yet produced actual life by building proteins. It is still rather difficult to even define life, let alone manufacture it. But we can sustain and give growth to living forms by proper feeding procedures.

The main objective in combining food factors is to mix them in the various amounts necessary to procure a balanced diet. This can be done in a number of ways. The essential difference in the many good methods of feeding lies in the time it takes to prepare the food and in the end cost of the materials used. Dogs can be fed expensively and they can be fed cheaply, and in each instance they can be fed equally well.

There are various food products on the market packaged specifically for canine consumption. The quality of these foods as complete diets in themselves ranges from poor to excellent. The better *canned*, or *pudding*, foods are good but expensive for feeding a number of dogs. Compact and requiring no preparation, the canned foods are fine for use at shows or when traveling— though for traveling an even better diet is biscuits, lean meat, and very little water. The result is less urination and defecation, since the residue from this diet is very small. The diet is, of course, not to be fed over any extended period of time because it lacks food-value.

Biscuits can be considered as tidbits rather than food, since much of the vitamin and mineral content has been destroyed by baking. The same holds true for *kibbled* foods. They are fillers to which must be added fat, milk, broths, meat, vegetables, and vitamin and mineral supplement.

By far the most complete of the manufactured foods are the *grain foods*. In such a highly competitive business as the manufacturing and merchandising of these foods, it is essential for the manufacturer to market a highly palatable and balanced ration. The better grain foods have constantly changing formulas to conform to the most recent results of scientific dietary research. They are, in many cases, the direct result of controlled generation tests in scientific kennels where their efficacy can be ascertained. A good grain food should not be considered merely a filler. Rather, it should be employed as the basic diet to which fillers might possibly be added. Since the grain food is bag or box packaged and not hermetically sealed, the fat content is necessarily low. A high degree of fat would produce quick rancidity. Therefore fat must be added to the dry food. Milk, which is one of the finest of foods in itself, can be added along with broths or plain warm water to arrive at the proper consistency for palatability. With such a diet we have a true balance of essentials, wastage is kept to a minimum, stools are small and firm and easily removed, and cost and labor have been reduced to the smallest equation possible to arrive at and yet feed well. The *pellet type* food is simply grain food to which a binding agent has been added to hold the grains together in the desired compact form.

Fat should be introduced into the dog's diet in its pure form. Proteins and carbohydrates are converted into fat by the body. Fat also causes the dog to retain his food longer in the stomach. It stores vitamins E, K, A, and D, and lessens the bulk necessary to be fed at each meal. Fat can be melted and poured over the meal, or put through the meat grinder and then mixed with the basic ration.

Just as selection is important in breeding, so ratio is important in feeding. The proper diet must not only provide all the essentials, it must also supply those essentials in the proper proportions. This is what we mean by a balanced diet. It can be dangerous to your Cocker's well being if the ratios of any of his dietary essentials are badly unbalanced over a period of time. The effects can be disastrous in the case of puppies. This is the basic reason for putting your faith in a good, scientifically balanced grain dog food.

There is an abundance of concentrated *vitamin supplements* on the market specifically manufactured for dogs. They are undoubtedly of real worth— if your dog needs a supplement. Dogs fed a balanced diet do not need additional concentrated supplements, with the exception, perhaps, of the rare individual. If you feel that your dog is in need of a supplement, it is wiser to consult your veterinarian for advice and specific dosage. Check the label of the dog food you buy to make sure that it has all the necessary ingredients. If it has, you will not find it necessary to pour in concentrated, highly expensive supplements. Another of the supplements widely in use today, packaged under various trade names, embodies the elements of what was initially called A.P.F., or animal protein factor. This is a powder combining various antibiotic residues with the composite vitamin B_{12}. The role of this supplement in dog feeding has not, as yet, been adequately established. Theoretically, it is supposed that this supplement produces better food utilization and the production of extra body fat, which accounts for better growth and weight. On the other hand, it is also thought that it can affect the normal balance of intestinal flora, and overdoses can produce undesirable effects. Nature is generally generous in her gift of vitamins, minerals, and

A quartette of various breeds of Spaniels that share the same basic genetic source as the Cocker Spaniel. Above is the Springer Spaniel and below, the Clumber Spaniel.

Above is the Spaniel most closely related to the Cocker, the English Cocker Spaniel. Below is a Sussex Spaniel, whose type is much like that of the earliest Cocker Spaniels.

other nutritional essentials, and all can be found, in adequate abundance, in the balanced diet. We do not want to rule out supplements, but we do want to stress that they should be used with care.

In many instances kennel owners feel that their animals, for various reasons, need a supplementary boost in their diet. Some are in critical stages of growth, bitches are about to be bred or are in whelp, mature dogs are being frequently used for stud, and others are recuperating from illness. In such cases supplements can be added to the food, but in reasonable amounts. It is better, too, to supply the supplements through the medium of natural nutritional material rather than chemical, concentrated, commercial supplements. Brewers' yeast, alfalfa meal, and similar natural agents can be mixed separately in a container and judicious quantities added to the basic diet.

Calcium and *phosphorus* in pure chemical form must be handled with care when used in the dog's diet. Toxic conditions can be caused by an over-abundance of this material in the bloodstream. Green, ground, edible bone meal is a much better product to use where it is thought necessary. Most good grain foods have an abundance of this inexpensive element in correct balance. Milk is a highly desirable vehicle for balanced calcium and phosphorus as well as many other nutritional needs.

Cod liver oil is another product that, if given to excess over a period of time, can cause toxidity and bone malformation. It is better and cheaper to employ a fish liver oil concentrate such as percomorph oil. In this oil the base vehicle has been discarded and the pure oil concentrated, so that a very small dosage is required. Many owners and breeders pour cod liver oil and throw handsful of calcium and supplementary concentrates into the food pans in such lavish amounts that there is a greater bulk of these than of the basic food, on the theory that, if a little does some good, a greater amount will be of immense benefit. This concept is both ridiculous and dangerous.

An occasional pinch of *bicarbonate of soda* in the food helps to neutralize stomach acidity and can prevent, or alleviate, fatigue caused by a highly acid diet. Bones need never be fed to dogs for food value if the diet is complete. Poultry bones should never be fed. They splinter into sharp shards which can injure gums or rip the throat lining or intestines. Once in the stomach they are dissolved by strong gastric juices. It is on their way to their ultimate goal that they do damage. The same is also true of fishbones. Soft rib bones are excellent to feed your dog periodically, not necessarily as nourishment, but to clean his teeth. The animals teeth pierce through them completely, and in so doing tartar will be removed and the teeth kept clean of residue. These soft rib bones can be considered the canine's toothbrush. Nylon and rawhide, manufactured bones serve the same purpose.

Table scraps are always good, and if your dog is a good eater and easy keeper, give him any leftovers in his food pan, including potatoes. The diets of good feeders can be varied to a greater extent without unfavorable repercussions than can the diets of finicky eaters. Fish is a good food, containing all the food elements which are found in meat, with a bonus of extra nutritional values. *Muscle meat* lacks many essentials and is so low in calcium that, even when supplemented with vitamin D, there is grave danger of rickets developing. In its raw state, meat is frequently the intermediate host of several forms of internal parasites. Meat by-products and canned meat, which generally contains by-products, are much better as food for dogs than pure muscle meat. Incidentally, whale meat, which is over 80 per cent protein, could well replace horse meat, which is less than 50 per cent protein, in the dog's diet.

Water is one of the elementary nutritional essentials. Considering the fact that the dog's body is approximately 70 per cent water, which is distributed in varying percentages throughout the body tissues and organs, including the teeth and bones, it isn't difficult to realize the importance of this staple to the dog's well being. Water flushes the system, stimulates gastric juice activity, brings about better appetite, and acts as a solvent within the body. It is one of the major sources of necessary minerals and helps during hot weather, and to a lesser degree during winter, to regulate the dogs temperature. When a dog is kept from water for any appreciable length of time, dehydration occurs. This is a serious condition, a fact which is known to any dog owner whose animal has been affected by diarrhea, continuous nausea, or any of the diseases in which this form of body shrinkage occurs.

Water is the cheapest part of your dog's diet, so supply it freely, particularly in warm weather. In winter if snow and ice are present and available to your Cocker, water is not so essential. At any rate, if left in a bucket in his run, it quickly turns to ice. Yet even under these conditions it is an easy matter to bring your dog in and supply him with at least one good drink of fresh water during the day. Being so easily provided, so inexpensive, and so highly essential to your Cocker's health, sober thought dictates that we should allow our dogs to "take to drink."

Breeders with only a few dogs can sometimes afford the extra time, expense, and care necessary to feed a varied and complicated diet. But it is easy to see that to feed a large kennel in such fashion would take an immense amount of time, labor, and expense. Actually, the feeding of a scientifically balanced grain food as the basic diet eliminates the element of chance which exists in diets prepared by the kennel owner from natural sources, since overabundance of some specific elements, as well as a lack of others, can bring about dietary ills and deficiencies.

Caloric requirements vary with age, temperament, changes in temperature, and activity. If your dog is nervous, very active, young, and kept out-of-doors in winter, his caloric intake must be greater than the phlegmatic,

A great red and white parti-color of some years back, Ch. Bar-Nan's Showman's Roderic. This nice stud was rich in the genetic background that built the fame of the Idahurst line.

underactive, fully grown dog who has his bed in the house. Keep your dog in good flesh, neither too fat nor too thin. You are the best judge of the amount to feed him to keep him in his best condition. A well-fed Cocker should always be in show "bloom"—clear-eyed, glossy-coated, filled with vim and vigor, and with enough of an all-over layer of fat to give him sleekness without plumpness.

FEEDING TECHNIQUES

The consistency of the food mix can vary according to your Cocker's taste. It is best not to serve the food in too sloppy a mixture, except in the case of very young puppies. It is also good practice to feed the same basic ration at every meal so that the taste of the food does not vary greatly at each feeding. Constant changing of the diet, with supplementary meals of raw or cooked meat, tends to produce finicky eaters, the bane of the kennel and private owners' existence. Never leave the food pan before your dog for more than thirty minutes. If he hasn't eaten by then, or has merely nibbled, the pan should be removed and not presented to him again until his next feeding time. This same policy should be followed when breaking a dog to a new diet. If he has become a canine gourmet, spoiled by a delicate diet, he may sometimes refuse to eat for two or three days. But eventually, when his hunger becomes acute enough and he realizes his hunger strike will not result in coddling and the bringing forth of his former delicacies, he will eat with gusto whatever is put before him. Remember, your Cocker is not a lap dog—he is an energetic sporting dog and should not be babied. Where there are several dogs to create mealtime competition, there is little danger of finicky eaters regardless of what is fed.

Keep your feeding utensils clean to eliminate the danger of bacterial for-

mation and sourness, especially in warm weather. Your food pans can be of any solid metal material. Agate, porcelain, and the various types of enamelware have a tendency to chip, and are therefore not desirable.

Every kennel owner and breeder has his own pet diet which has proven successful in the rearing and maintenance of his stock. In each instance he will insist that his is the only worth-while diet, and he cannot be blamed for so asserting, since his particular diet has nourished and kept his own stock in top condition over a period of years. Yet the truth is, as we have mentioned before in this chapter, that there are many ways to feed dogs and feed them well, and no one diet can be said to be the best.

Remember always that feeding ranks next to breeding in the influence it exerts on the growing dog. Knowledgeable breeding can produce genetically fine specimens, selection can improve the strain and the breed, but, without full and proper nourishment, particularly over the period of growth, the dog cannot attain to the promise of his heritage. The brusque slogan of a famous cattle breeder might well be adopted by breeders of Cockers. The motto is, "Breed, feed, weed."

Correct grooming of your Cocker Spaniel takes knowledge and acquired skill. Constant care will pay off in health and beauty, for the Cocker, like any other breed, needs specific coat care and grooming.

VI

General Care

When you own a dog, you own a dependent. Though the Internal Revenue Department does not recognize this fact, it is nevertheless true. Whatever pleasure one gets out of life must be paid for in some kind of coin, and this is as applicable to the pleasure we derive from our dogs as it is in all things. With our dogs we pay the toll of constant care. This Cocker which you have taken into your home and made a part of your family life depends completely upon you for his every need. In return for the care you give him, he repays you with a special brand of love and devotion that can't be duplicated. That is the bargain you make with your dog: your care on one side of the scale, his complete idolatry on the other. Not quite a fair bargain, but we humans, unlike our dogs, are seldom completely fair and unselfish.

Good husbandry pays off in dollars and cents too, particularly if you have more than one or two dogs, or run a semicommercial kennel. Clean, well-cared for dogs are most often healthy dogs, free from parasitic invaders and the small ills that bring other and greater woes in their wake. Good feeding and proper exercise help build strength and resistance to disease, and a sizable run keeps your canine friend from wandering into the path of some speeding car. Veterinarian bills and nursing time are substantially reduced, saving you money and time, when your dog is properly cared for.

Cleanliness, that partner to labor which is owned by some to be next to Godliness, is the first essential of good dog care. This applies to the dog's surrounding environment as well as to the dog himself. If your Cocker sleeps in the house, provide him with a draft-free spot for his bed, away from general household traffic. This bed can be a piece of rug or a well-padded dog mattress. It doesn't particularly matter what material is used as long as it is kept clean and put in the proper place.

Feeding has been comprehensively discussed in the previous chapter, but the utensils used and the methods of feeding come more specifically under the heading of general care, so we will repeat these few facts mentioned in the previous chapter. Heavy aluminium feeding pans are best, since they are easily cleaned and do not chip as does agate or porcelain. Feed your dog regularly in the same place and at the same time. Establish a friendly and quiet atmosphere during feeding periods and do not coax him to eat. If he refuses the food or nibbles at it sparingly, remove his food and do not feed again until the next feeding period. Never allow a pan of food to stand before a healthy dog for more than thirty minutes under any circumstances. Should your Cocker's appetite continue to be off, consult your veterinarian for the cause.

If you are feeding several dogs in an outside kennel, it is good practice to remain until all are finished, observing their appetites and eating habits while you wait. Often two dogs, kenneled together and given the same amount and kind of food, show different results. One will appear thin and the other in good condition. Sometimes the reason is a physiological one, but more often observation will show that the thinner dog is a slower eater than his kennel mate; that the latter dog gulps down his own food and then drives the thin dog away from his food pan before his ration is fully consumed and finishes this extra portion, too.

Never, never, force feed a healthy dog simply because he refuses an occasional meal. Force feeding and coaxing make finicky eaters and a finicky feeder is never in good coat or condition and turns feeding time into the most exasperating experience of the day. Rather than forcing or coaxing, it is better to starve your dog, showing no sympathy at all when he refuses food. If he is healthy, he will soon realize that he will experience hunger unless he eats when the food pan is put before him and will soon develop a normal and healthy appetite. Immediately upon removing the food pans, they should be thoroughly washed and stacked, ready for the next mealtime.

During hot weather, be certain that your dog has a constant supply of fresh, clean water. In winter, water left outside in runs will freeze solid and be of no use to the dogs, so it is best to provide fresh water two or three times a day and remove the pail after the dogs have had their fill. Always provide water within an hour after feeding.

It has been the experience of most dog people that animals kept or kenneled outdoors, both winter and summer, are healthier and in better condition generally than their softer living housedog brethren. Light and the seasons have a great deal to do with shedding and coat condition. The outdoor dog, living in an environment approaching the natural, has regular shedding periods, after which his new coat comes in hard, strong, and glossy. Housedogs living in conditions of artificial light and heat seem to shed constantly, and seldom possess the good coat exhibited by the dog who lives outdoors. The housedog is much more susceptible to quick changes in temperature, particularly in the winter when he is brought from a warm, furnace-heated house, into the frigid out-of-doors. Never forget that your Cocker is a sporting dog, not a lap dog, and treat him accordingly. Babying an individual of a breed of such high intelligence can produce a nuisance or a canine hypochondriac.

PLANNING YOUR RUN

Even the housedog should be provided with an outside run and house, a domain of his own to keep him in the sun and air and protect him from disturbance by children or other dogs. There, in his run, he is safe from accident, and you know he can't run away to become lost, strayed, or stolen. There, also, you can be sure he is not soiling or digging in your neighbor's newly planted lawn, a situation which can strain, to put it mildly, any "good-neighbor policy." Provide shade in some section of the run against the hot summer sun. Natural shade from trees is the ideal, of course, but artificial shade can be provided by a canvas overthrow placed strategically.

The run should be as large as your property will permit. Six by fifteen feet is a good size for one to four dogs, but if space permits it, a longer run is preferable. If you are building a kennel of several runs, remember that the length is more important than the width, and connecting runs in a row can be cut down in width if the length provided is ample.

The best surface for your run is a question open for argument. Some breeders prefer packed-down fine cinders for their run surface, claiming that this material provides good drainage and is the best surface for a dog's feet, keeping them compact and strong. Actually, heredity and, to a lesser degree, diet, are the prime factors that produce good feet in dogs, but a dog's feet will spread and lose compactness if he is kept constantly on a soft or muddy surface. Cinders do make an excellent run, but this surface also makes an admirable place in which parasitic eggs and larvae can exist and thrive, and they are almost impossible to clean out from such a surface, short of resorting to a blowtorch. Others favor cement runs. They are easy to clean and present a good appearance. But again, we have a porous surface into which the minute eggs of parasites can take refuge. Only by daily scrubbing with a strong disinfectant, or periodic surface burning, can concrete runs be kept free of parasitic eggs and larvae.

Gravel and plain dirt runs present the same disadvantage, plus the difficulty of efficiently gathering stools from such surfaces. Dirt runs also become muddy in rainy weather and dusty in dry weather, making it necessary to change bedding often, and producing, as formerly mentioned, a deleterious effect upon the animal's feet. It would seem, then, that none of these run surfaces is the perfect answer to our problem. But there is yet another run

American and Canadian Champion, Condoro Call Me Charlie, B.O.V. at American Spaniel Club, 1966, owned by Dorothy L. Conway and Bill Ernst.
sire: Ch. Maindales Mr. Success
dam: Champagnes Creation

surface which can give us better control over parasitic reinfestation. On this run we employ washed builders' sand for the surface. The dog generally defecates in a limited area, almost always at the end of his run farthest from the run door and his own house. Stools can easily be removed from the sand surface, and by digging down and removing one or two inches of sand below the stool, parasitic invaders are also removed. Fresh sand is filled into the spaces left by cleaning. The sand soon packs down and becomes a solid surface. The grains drop easily from the dog's feet and are not carried into his house to soil his bedding. This sand is not expensive, and periodically the whole surface can be removed and fresh sand brought in and leveled.

An ideal run would be one with a cement base which can be washed down with disinfectants or a strong borax solution (which will destroy hookworm larvae) whenever the surface sand is completely removed and before a fresh sand surface is provided.

A portable, outdoor wire pen that can be put any place on the lawn and can be carried with you in a station wagon. These portable pens are useful and very handy to have; keeping your dog or dogs safe from harm.

BUILDING YOUR RUN

If you plan to build the run yourself, you might consider the "soil-cement" surface as a base rather than true cement. Soil-cement is a subsurface employed on light-traffic airfields and many suburban roads; it is inexpensive, durable, and easily built without special knowledge or equipment. First remove the sod on the area to be converted into a run, then loosen the soil to a depth of about four inches with a spade and pulverize the soil, breaking up any lumps with a rake. Scatter dry cement at the rate of two-thirds of a sack of cement to a square yard of surface and mix in thoroughly with the soil until the mixture has a floury texture. Adjust your hose to a mist spray and water the surface until the soil-cement mixture will mold under pressure, and not crumble. Follow by raking the entire mixture to full depth to assure uniform moisture, and level at the same time. Now you must work quickly,

A section of an indoor kennel showing several dogs in individual open wire crates and one aluminum closed crate. A garage can be easily converted into a place for dogs similar to this. Of course dogs cannot be kept too long in such small enclosures.

compacting the run with a tamper and then rolling with a garden roller. All this must be done within a half-hour or the surface will harden while still uneven. After rolling, the surface should be smooth and even. Mist-spray again, then cover with a coating of damp sawdust or soil for a week, after which the run can be used. Remember to keep a slight slope on all run surfaces so that water can drain off without puddling. Soil-cement is also excellent for paths around, or to and from, the kennels.

CLEANING YOUR RUN

In removing stools from a run, never rake them together first. This practice tends to spread worm eggs over a greater area. Shovel each stool up separately, and deposit it in a container. When the run is clean, carry the container to a previously prepared pit, dump the contents, and cover with a layer of dirt. Hose out the container and apply disinfectant, and the job is done with a minimum of bother. In winter, due to snow and ice, very little can be done about run sanitation. But those who live in climates which have definite and varied seasons have the consolation of knowing that worm eggs do not incubate nor fleas develop during cold weather. Therefore they must only do whatever is possible in run cleanliness for the sake of appearance and to keep down odors.

FENCING YOUR RUN

Fencing the run is our next problem. The ideal fencing is heavy chain link with metal supporting posts set in cement, and erected by experts. But if your pocketbook cries at such an expenditure (and the cost is not small), you can do your own fencing, cutting the cost drastically by purchasing cheaper wire, using cedar posts for supports, and girding your loins for a bit of labor. Hog wire, $1\frac{1}{2}''$ fox wire, or heavy poultry wire all can be used. Whatever fencing you employ, be sure it is high enough and is of a heavy enough gauge to be substantial. Dig post holes, using horizontally stretched string as a guide to keep them evenly in line, and dig them deeply enough to hold the posts securely. Leave approximately six feet of space between each post hole. Paint the section of the post which is to be buried in the hole with creosote, or some other good wood preservative and set the posts in the holes. Concrete and rock, poured into the hole around the post, will provide a firm base. A horizontal top rail strengthens the run materially and will make for a better job. Brace all corner and gate posts as shown in the illustration. When your posts are in and set, borrow a wire stretcher for use in applying the wire fencing to the posts. This handy instrument can make the difference between a poor and a good job.

Diagramatic line drawing of a kennel run corner post.

side brace

ground line

main corner post

wire below surface

cement corner post support

The fine red dog, Ch. Jo Be Glen's Bronze Falcon, owned by Mrs. Charles Schlang, shown here being handled to a nice win at the C.S.C. of R.I. by Ted Young, Jr.

COCKER SPANIEL
CLUB OF RHODE ISLAND
NOV. 3, 1962
BEST OF BREED
IN SHOW
JUDGE - MRS. WM. HENRY

PLANS FOR A DOG HOUSE

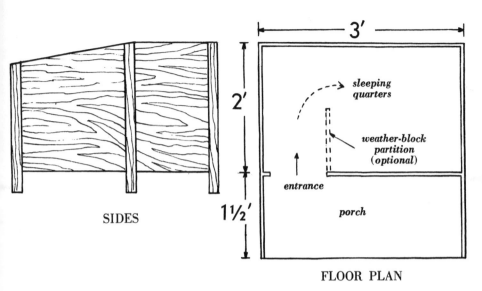

SIDES

2'

1½'

3'

sleeping
quarters

weather-block
partition
(*optional*)

entrance

porch

FLOOR PLAN

FINISHED HOUSE

E.H.H.

YOUR DOG HOUSE

The dog house can be simple or elaborate, reaching the extremes from a barrel set on cement blocks, to a miniature human dwelling, complete with shingles and windows. The best kind of house comes somewhere in between these two extremes. Build the house large enough, with sleeping quarters approximately 3 by 2 feet, and 2 feet high at the highest point. Incorporate a front porch $1\frac{1}{2}$ feet deep on the front of the house. If the house is correctly situated, the porch roof offers shade from the sun and the porch itself a place to lie in rainy or snowy weather. Make the skeleton framework of one by twos, first building the two side sections, allowing three inches of extra height on the uprights for floor elevation. Incorporate the porch size in the over-all length of the side pieces and remember the back slope over the sleeping portion, which will accommodate the hinged roof.

Next build the floor frame and cover it with three-eights-inch outdoor plywood, or tongue and groove siding. Cover the sides with the same material you use for the floor. If you allow your two-by-three-inch framing to show on the outside of the house, you will have a smooth inner surface to attach your floor platform to. Keep the floor the three inches above ground level provided by your side uprights and brace the floor by nailing three-inch pieces under the floor and to the inside bottom of the side uprights. Frame in the door section between the porch and the sleeping quarters, framing for a door up from the floor to hold in the bedding. Nail your plywood, or tongue and groove siding, over this framework, of course leaving the opening for the door, and nail the same wood across the back and the porch roof, thus closing the house in all around except for the roof section over the sleeping quarters. Build this section separately, with an overlay on the two sides and the back. Attach an underneath flange of wood on both sides and the rear, in from the edges, so that the flanges will fit snugly along the three outside edges of the house proper to keep out drafts and cold. Hinge this roof section to the back edge of the porch roof and cover the entire roof part with shingles or heavy tar paper, with a separate flap stripped along and covering the hinged edge. Paint the house (blue or blue-gray paint is said to discourage flies), and it is finished.

If you wish, you may insulate with board insulation on the inside, or double flooring can be provided with insulating paper between the layers. In cold weather a gunny sack or a piece of canvas, rug or blanket, should be tacked at the top edge of the doorway to fall across the opening, thus blocking out cold air. If the house is big enough, an inside partial wall can be provided at one side of the door, essentially dividing the inner portion into a front hall with a weather-blocking partition between this hall and the sleeping quarters. If you build the house without the porch, you will find it necessary to build a separate platform on which the dog can lie outside in the sun after snow or rain. Should your ambitions embrace a full-sized kennel building with office, etc., it might be wise to investigate the prefabricated kennel buildings which are now on the market.

This house that you build, because of its size, is not an easy thing to handle or carry, so we suggest that you build it as close to the site you have picked for it as possible. The site should be at the narrow end of the run, with just a few inches of the porch jutting into the run and the greater bulk of the house outside of the run proper. Situate the house at the door end of the run, so that when you approach the run, the dog will not track through his excreta, which will be distributed at the end of the run farthest from the door. Try to set the house with its side to the north and back to the west. This gives protection from the coldest compass point in winter and shades the porch in summer from the hot afternoon sun.

A house built to the dimensions advised will accommodate two fully grown Cockers comfortably. Remember that the smaller and lower you can build your house without cramping your dog, the warmer it will be in the winter. If the house is not too large, is well built, and the doorway blocked adequately, you will be surprised by the amount of heat the dog's body will generate in cold weather to keep his sleeping quarters warm. To house several dogs, the necessary number of houses can be built or, if you so wish, one house doubled in length, with a dividing partition and two doorways, to service two separate runs.

Bedding for the sleeping box can consist of marsh grass, oat, rye, or wheat straw, or wood, pine, or cedar shavings. The latter is said to discourage fleas and lice and possesses an aromatic odor. If any of the other materials are used, shake a liberal supply of flea powder in the bedding once a week or each time the bedding is changed. The bedding may be changed once a month, but should be changed more often in rainy or muddy weather. Old bedding should be burned so it will not become a breeding place for parasites. Periodically the dog house should be cleaned out, washed with soap and water and a good disinfectant, and aired with the hinged roof section propped open.

GROOMING

Grooming should be a pleasant experience and a time of silent and delightful communication between you and your dog. Try to find the time to groom your dog once every day. It should take only a few minutes of your time, except during the season of shedding. By removing dead hair, dust, and skin scales in the daily grooming, you keep your Cocker's coat glossy, his appearance neat. This kind of daily grooming also eliminates the necessity

*Try to find the time to groom your dog every day.
It should not be a chore. Rather should it be a
time of close communication for you and your
dog, a time that will establish a rapport between
you, and incidentally a way of keeping your dog
neat and clean and nice to be near.*

*The top black dog, Ch. Mijo's Momentum owned
by Mrs. Violet Myshrall, going Best in Show at
the Penn Ridge Kennel Club, August 1965,
under judge, Miss G. Groskin.
The handler is Ted Young, Jr*

of frequent bathings. For ordinary grooming use a metal comb with a handle. A comb of this sort permits you to dig below the surface of the outer coat. Be careful not to irritate the skin or pull out the undercoat. After combing thoroughly, go over the dog with a wire grooming glove and finish with a stiff-bristled brush. The preparation, grooming, clipping and beautifying your dog for show ring competition is completely covered in the chapter headed, Training Your Cocker For the Show Ring, which chapter also will tell you all you want to know about entering your dog and the meaning of the various dog show classes.

BATHING

You may bathe your dog or puppy any time you think it necessary, as long as you do not think it is necessary too frequently. Be careful in chilly weather to bathe him in a warm room and make sure he is completely dry before you allow him to venture out into the cold outdoors. When you bathe your dog, you soak him down to the skin and remove the protective oils from his coat. When a dog is exposed to rain and snow, the dampness is shed by the outer coat and kept from the skin by his undercoat. Therefore he is not likely to be affected by natural seasonal conditions. Be careful, however, that he is not exposed to these same conditions directly after a bath, as there is danger of his contracting a cold. During the time of shedding, a bath once a week is not too often if the weather is warm. It helps to remove loose hair and skin scales, as does the grooming that should follow the bath when the dog is completely dry. As mentioned above, your dog's coat is water-resistant, so the easiest way to insure the removal of deep dirt and odors caused by accumulated sebum is by employing a chemicalized liquid soap with a coconut-oil base. Some commercial dog soaps contain vermin poisons, but an occasional prepared vermicidal dip, after bathing and rinsing, is more effective and very much worth while. When bathing, rub the lather in strongly down to the skin, being careful not to get soap in the dog's eyes. Cover every inch of him with heavy lather, rub it in, scrape the excess off with your hands, rinse and dry thoroughly, then walk him in the sun until he is ready for grooming. There are paste soaps available that require no rinsing, making the bathing of your Cocker that much easier, or you may wish to use liquid detergents manufactured specifically for canine bathing. Prepared canned lathers, as well as dry shampoos, are all available at pet shops and are all useful in keeping your dog clean and odorless.

If your dog has walked in tar which you find you cannot remove by bathing, you can remove it with kerosene. The kerosene should be quickly removed with strong soap and water if it is not to burn and irritate the skin. Paint can be washed off with turpentine, which must also be quickly removed for the same reasons. Some synthetic paints, varnishes, enamels, and other like preparations, which are thinned with alcohol, can be removed by the same vehicle. If the paint (oil base) is close to the skin, linseed oil will dissolve it without irritation. Should your Cocker engage in a tête-à-tête with a skunk, wash him immediately (if you can get near him) with soap and hot water, or soak him with tomato juice if you can find enough available, then walk him in the hot sun. The odor evaporates most quickly under heat.

A box of small sticks with cotton-tipped ends, which are manufactured under various brand names, are excellent for cleaning your Cocker's ears. Drop into the ear a mixture of ether and alcohol, or of propylene glycol, to dissolve dirt and wax, then swab the ear clean with the cotton-tipped stick. Surplus liquid will quickly evaporate.

CARE OF NAILS AND TEETH

Keep your dog's claws trimmed short. Overgrown nails cause lameness, foot ailments, spread toes, and hare feet. If your dog does a great deal of walking on cement, nail growth is often kept under control naturally by wearing off on the cement surface. Some Cocker's seem to possess a genetic factor for short claws which never need trimming, but the majority of our dogs need nail care. To accomplish this task with the least possible trouble, use a nail-cutter specifically designed for use on dogs and cut away only the horny dead section. If you cut too deeply, you will cause bleeding. A flashlight held under the nail will enable you to see the dark area of the

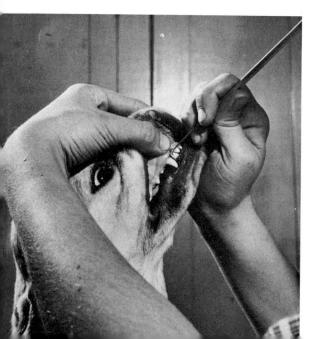

Forming tartar should be scraped from your dog's teeth. Most owners prefer to have their veterinarian do this chore.

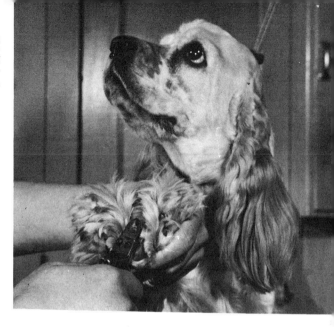

Clipping the nails is easy, and necessary for good foot care. A special type of dog nail clipper should be employed.

blood line so you can avoid cutting into it. If you should tap the blood supply in the claw don't be overly alarmed, simply keep the dog quiet until the severed capillaries close and the bleeding stops. Munsel's solution or a styptic pencil applied to the bleeding claw helps to hurry coagulation. After you have cut the nails, file them smooth with the use of a nail file. File from above with a downward, rounding stroke. If a nail has bled from trimming, do not file it for at least twenty-four hours.

Artificial bones given twice a week will help prevent tartar from forming on your dog's teeth. His teeth pierce the bones, scraping off tooth residue in the process, keeping his teeth clean and white. If tartar should form, it can be chipped off with the same kind of instrument your dentist uses on your teeth for that purpose, or your veterinarian can clean them efficiently and without bother to you. Check your dog's mouth every other week for broken, loose, or abscessed teeth, particularly when he has passed his prime. Bad teeth must be tended by your veterinarian before they affect your dog's general health.

FLIES

During the summer months certain flies, commonly called "deer" flies, bite at the ears causing great discomfort, the formation of scabs, subsequent baldness, and sometimes infection in that area. A good liquid insecticide, one of the many recently developed for fly control, should be rubbed or sprayed on the dog's ears as often as necessary to keep these pests away.

Skin-disease salve which contains sulphur and oil of turpentine as a vehicle is also efficacious against flies, particularly if D.D.T. flea powder is shaken on top of the salve, where it adheres, giving extra protection. Oil of Benzoin and oil of Cade, painted on the ears, are also effective.

RATS

If rats invade the kennel area, they should be eradicated as quickly as possible. Not only are they disease carriers, but they are an affront to our more delicate senses. To get rid of them, set out small pans of dog meal near their holes every night for several nights until you have them coming to these pans to feed. Then mix Red Squill with the dog food they are being fed, eight measures of dog meal to one of Red Squill. After a single night's feeding of this poisonous mixture, you will generally rid your premises of these gray marauders. Red Squill is a drug that is nonpoisonous to all animals except rodents, so it can be used around the kennel with safety.

TRAVEL

When traveling in hot weather with your dog, never leave him in a closed car in the sun alone. Death takes its grisly toll each summer of dogs so treated. Carry his water pail and food dish with you and take care of his needs as you do your own when on the road. If you intend changing his diet to one more easily fed when traveling, begin the change a few days before your trip so he can become accustomed to it. Gaines Research Division publishes a list of approximately 3,500 hostelries across the country that will accept dogs—a handy booklet for the dog-loving traveler to have.

If you find it necessary to ship a Cocker to another section of the country, make sure the crate you use is large enough in all dimensions to keep the dog from being cramped during his journey. Check to see that there are no large openings or weak sections which might break in transit and allow the dog's limbs to project out of the crate. Consult your veterinarian or your local express agency for data on state health certificates. Supply the dog with a pan, rigidly attached to the crate, for water, and throw a few dog biscuits on the floor of the crate for the dog to gnaw during his journey to alleviate boredom. Be sure there are air holes in strategic locations to provide air and ventilation. If possible, the top surface of the crate should be rounded, rather than flat, to discourage the parking of other crates on top of the dog crate. Strips of wood, nailed horizontally along the outside of the crate and projecting out from the surface, will prevent adjacent crates, or boxes, from being jammed tightly against the dog crate and thus blocking and defeating the purpose of the ventilation holes.

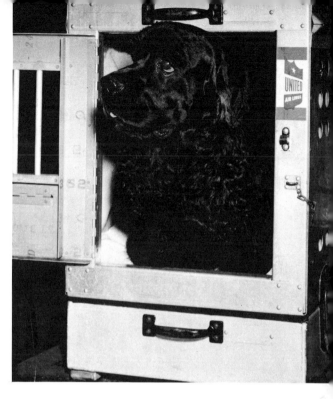

A Cocker in a shipping crate. Such crates can be made of wood or aluminum. If you are shipping a dog by air a suitable crate can be rented from the airline you select.

A periodic health check of your Cocker by your veterinarian can pay big mental and monetary dividends. When you take him for his examination, remember to bring with you samples of his stool and urine for analysis.

EXERCISE

Your Cocker needs a good deal of exercise if he is to be in good physical shape and not become fat. The hunting Cocker generally has enough and the right kind of exercise if he is used consistently during the hunting season. At other times many field Cockers are allowed to hunt by themselves, the theory being that it keeps them keen and any bad form they may develop can be corrected. The exercise they get from this is certainly worthwhile and beneficial.

The show dog of course needs lots of good exercise to keep his flesh and muscles tight, his gait swinging and his eyes bright. Throwing a ball or a stick for him to retrieve is ideal exercise coupled with nice long walks. This will also be of benefit to you for most of us tend to eat too much and exercise too little.

The owner of the pet dog should be just as attentive to this facet of canine husbandry. Even though your Cocker is not a gun dog or a show dog, he still needs adequate exercise to continue being a good pet and companion. Without exercise he will become fat and lazy and not as capable of combating disease. The same kind of exercise recommended for the show dog is fine for the pet dog too.

We have considered in this chapter the elements of physical care, but we must not forget that your Cocker needs mental care as well. His character and mental health need nourishment, grooming, and exercise, just as much as his physical being. Give him your companionship and understanding,

A Percy Jones portrait of three champion Penrock Cockers. From left to right they are, Ch. Penrock's Personality, Ch. Penrock's Jennifer, and Ch. Penrock's Perfection.

teach him right from wrong, and treat him as you would a friend whom you enjoy associating with. This, too, is a part of his general care, and perhaps the most important part for both you and your dog.

Remember that good general care is the first and most important part of canine ownership and disease prevention. The health and happiness of your Cocker is in your hands. A small amount of labor each day by those hands is your dog's health and life insurance, and the premium is paid by your Cocker in love and devotion.

Above is the parti, Ch. Smokey
Sentinal, who also sported the
C.D.X. title after his name.

Center is
Ch. Lucknow Leading Lady, a lovely
bitch by Midkiff Kermit x Midkiff
Sylvie.

Below is depicted the fine
old show and stud dog,
Ch. Nonquitt Nowanda's Noel.

The brood bitch is the basis upon which a
breeding kennel survives or falls. The good brood
bitch above is Champel's Certainly Sumpin', by
Ch. Crackerbox Certainly x Champel's Caress,
C.D. With her are her two eight-week old sons
sired by Ch. Valli-Lo's Flash A'Way. Owner-
breeder of dam and puppies is Elizabeth
H. Ahrens.

VII

The Brood Bitch

If we want to succeed in improvement within our breed, we must have an even greater trueness to breed type in our bitches than we have in their breeding partners. The productive value of the bitch is comparatively limited in scope by seasonal vagary and this, in turn, increases the importance of every litter she produces.

To begin breeding, we must of necessity, begin with a bitch as the foundation. The foundation of all things must be strong and free from faults, or the structure we build upon it will crumble. The bitch we choose for our foundation bitch must, then, be a good bitch, as fine as we can possibly acquire, not in structure alone, but in mentality and character as well. She is a product of her germ plasm, and this most important facet of her being must be closely analyzed so that we can compensate, in breeding, for her hidden faults. Structurally, the good brood bitch should be strongly made and up to standard size. She should be deep and not too long in body, for overlong bitches are generally too long in loin and weak in back, and after a litter tend to sag in back line. She must possess good bone strength throughout, yet she should not be so coarse as to lack femininity. Weakness and delicacy are not the essence of femininity in our breed and should be particularly avoided in the brood bitch.

THE PERIOD OF HEAT

Your bitch will first come in season when she is between seven and eleven months of age. Though this is an indication that nature considers her old enough and developed enough to breed, it is best to allow her to pass this first heat and plan to breed her when she next comes in season. This should come within six months if her environment remains the same. Daylight, which is thought to affect certain glands, seems to occasionally influence the ratio of time between heats, as will complete change in environment.

Scientific studies of the incidence of seasonal variation in the mating cycles of bitches indicates that more bitches come in heat and are bred during the months of February through May than at any other time of year. The figures might not be completely reliable, since they were assembled through birth registrations in the A.K.C., and many breeders refrain from fall and winter breedings so they will not have winter or early spring litters.

Some breeders claim a bitch should not be bred until she has passed two seasons, but it is not necessary to wait this long. In fact, should you breed your bitch at her second season, it will probably be better for her, settling her in temperament and giving her body greater maturity and grace.

When your bitch is approaching her period of heat and you intend to breed her, have her stool checked for intestinal parasites, and if any are present, worm her. Feed her a well-balanced diet, such as she should have been getting all along. Her appetite will increase in the preparatory stage of the mating cycle as her vulva begins to swell. She will become restless, will urinate more frequently, and will allow dogs to approach her, but will not allow copulation. Within the bitch other changes are taking place at this stage. Congestion begins in the reproductive tract, the horns of the uterus and the vagina thicken, and the luteal bodies leave the ovaries.

The first sign of blood from the vulva ushers in the second stage of the mating cycle. In some bitches no blood appears at all, or so little that it goes unnoticed by the owner, and sometimes we find a bitch who will bleed throughout the cycle. In either circumstances we must depend upon other signs. The bitch becomes very playful with animals of her own and the opposite sex, but will still not permit copulation. This is, of course, a condition

BREEDING CYCLE OF THE BITCH

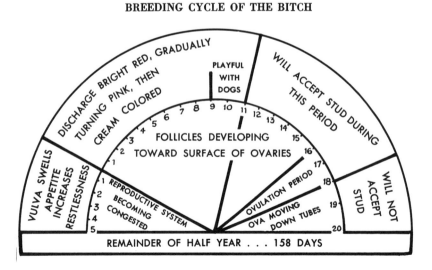

REMAINDER OF HALF YEAR . . . 158 DAYS

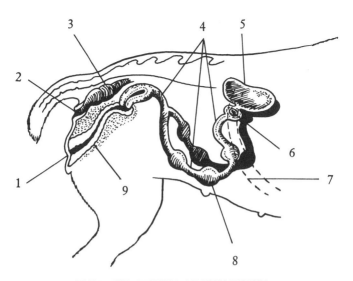

REPRODUCTIVE SYSTEM OF THE BITCH

1. Vulva 2. Anus 3. Rectum 4. Uterus 5. Kidney 6. Ovary 7. Ribs (indicated)
8. Developing embryo 9. Vagina

which is very trying to male dogs with which she comes in contact. Congestion within the bitch reaches a high point during this period. Ova develop within the follicles of the ovaries, and, normally, the red discharge gradually turns to pink, becoming lighter in color until it becomes straw color and is no longer obvious. Her vulva is more swollen, and she becomes increasingly more playful with males. This period is generally of about ten days' duration, but the time varies greatly with the individual. Rather than rely upon any set time period, it is best to conclude that this period reaches its conclusion when the bitch will stand for the stud and permit copulation. This generally occurs at about the tenth day, but can take place as early as the fourth or fifth day of this period or as late as the seventeenth day.

The third period in the cycle is the acceptance period. The bitch will swing her hind end toward the dog, her tail will arch up and stand high, and she will permit copulation. Sometimes the stud may have to tease her for a time, but she will eventually give in. The bitch may be sensitive and yelp and pull away when the stud's penis touches the lining of the vagina. If this occurs several times, it is best to wait another day, until the sensitivity has left this region. A very definite indication that the bitch is in the acceptance period is the softness and flaccidity of the vulva, from which the firmness and congestion has gone. Within the bitch the ovarian follicles have been growing ever bigger, and approximately midway in the acceptance period, some of them burst and the eggs are ready for fertilization. If the bitch has a normal mating cycle, as shown on the diagram, the best time to breed her is about the thirteenth or fourteenth day of the mating cycle, when ovulation has occurred. This time also varies with the individual bitch, so that until you have bred your bitch once or twice and feel that you know the best time for her, it is better to breed her on the eleventh day and every other day thereafter until her period of acceptance is over. This last, of course, is generally only possible when the stud is owned by you. One good breeding is actually all that is necessary to make your bitch pregnant, providing that

*Introducing the dog and bitch before breeding.
Do not rush them, allow them first to become
acquainted.*

breeding is made at the right time. If copulation is forced before the bitch is ready, the result is no conception or a small litter, since the sperm must wait for ovulation and the life of the sperm is limited. The acceptance period ceases rather abruptly, and is signaled by the bitch's definite resistance to male advances.

HANDLING THE MATING

If your bitch is a maiden, it is best to breed her this first time to an older stud who knows his business. When you bring her to the stud and if there

If either the dog or bitch (it is generally the bitch) show any inclination to bite or fight the proposed mate, the leash can be looped around its foreface, as shown in the photo, in lieu of a commercial muzzle, to keep it from injuring its partner.

are adjoining wire-enclosed runs, put the stud in one run and the bitch in the adjacent one. They will make overtures through the wire and later, when the stud is loosed in the run with the bitch, copulation generally occurs quickly. You may have to hold the bitch if she is flighty or reluctant, sometimes a problem with maiden bitches. If your bitch fails to conceive from a good and proper breeding, do not immediately put the blame on the stud. In most instances it is the fault of either the bitch or the owner of the bitch, who has not adequately timed the mating. Many bitch owners fail to recognize the first signs of the mating cycle and so bring their bitch to the stud either too early or too late. Normal physiology of the reproductive system can be interrupted or delayed by disturbance, disease, or illness in any part of the dog's body. A sick bitch will therefore generally not come in season, though it is time to do so, until after she has completely recovered and returned to normal. Bitches past their prime and older tend to have a shorter mating cycle and so must be bred sooner than usual to assure pregnancy.

During copulation and the resulting tie, you should assist the stud dog owner as much as possible. If the stud evidences pain when he attempts to force his penis in the vulva, check the bitch. In virgin bitches you may find a web of flesh which runs vertically across the vaginal opening and causes pain to the dog when his penis is forced against it. This web must be broken by hooking your finger around it and pulling if a breeding is to be consummated. After the tense excitement of the breeding and while the tie is in effect, speak to the bitch quietly and keep her from moving until the tie is broken, then snap a leash onto her collar and take her for a fast walk around the block without pausing. After that she can be taken home in the car. If it is necessary to travel any great distance before she arrives again in familiar surroundings, it is best to allow her a period of quiet rest before attempting the journey.

FALSE PREGNANCY

Occasionally fertile bitches, whether bred or not, will have false pregnancies and show every physical manifestation of true gestation up to the last moment. In some cases a bitch may be truly bred and then, after a month, resorb her fetuses. The only way of differentiating between pseudo-pregnancy and fetal resorbtion is by palpation, or feeling with the hands, to locate the fetal lump in the uterus. This is a difficult task for one who has not had vast experience.

PRE NATAL CARE

After you have returned home with your bitch, do not allow any males near her. She can become impregnated by a second dog and whelp a litter of mixed paternity, some of the puppies sired by the first dog and others

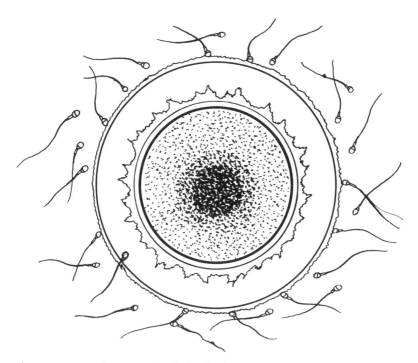

An egg, a special giant cell which the female ovaries produce, is here being assaulted by sperm which are attempting to pierce the envelope that surrounds the egg. The dark nucleus is the seat of the chromosomes, of which only half the required number are present. The first sperm to enter and reach the nucleus will bring with it the other necessary chromosomes for a normal cell number. Once inside the ovum the sperm will lose its tail. The nucleus of the egg is surrounded by growth enzymes.

sired by the second animal. Often a bitch is bred to a selected stud just before ovulation. The sperm will live long enough to fertilize the eggs when they flush down. The next day, another male breeds to the bitch, the sperm of the two dogs mix within her and both become sires of the resulting litter.

Let us assume that your bitch is in good health and you have had a good breeding to the stud of your choice at the proper time in the bitch's mating cycle to insure pregnancy. The male sperm fertilizes the eggs and life begins. From this moment on you will begin to feed the puppies which will be born in about sixty to sixty-three days from ovulation. Every bit of food you give the bitch is nutritionally aiding in the fetal development within her. Be sure that she is being provided with enough milk to supply calcium, meat for phosphorus and iron, and all the other essential vitamins and minerals. A vitamin and mineral supplement may be incorporated into the food if used moderately. Alfalfa leaf meal of 24 per cent protein content should

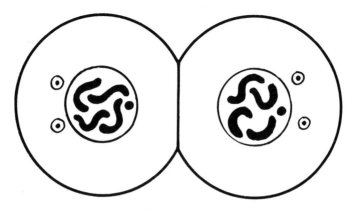

The cell is about to complete division and become two cells. The spindle has vanished, its job done. A nucleus appears in each of the cells in which there now is a complete set of chromosomes and two centrioles (for each cell). Each cell is now complete and perfect in itself, capable, and soon ready, to divide again.

become part of the diet. She must be fed well for her own maintenance and for the development of the young *in utero*, particularly during the last thirty days of the gestation period. She should not, however, be given food to such excess that she becomes fat.

Your bitch, her run, and house or bed should be free of worm and flea eggs. She should be allowed a moderate amount of free exercise in the pre-natal period to keep her from becoming fat and soft and from losing muscular tone and elasticity. If your bitch has not had enough exercise prior to breeding and you wish to harden and reduce her, accustom her to the exercise gradually and it will do her a great deal of good. But do not allow her to indulge in unaccustomed, abrupt, or violent exercise, or she might abort.

The puppies develop in the horns of the uterus, not in the "tubes" (Fallopian tubes), as is commonly thought. As the puppies develop, the horns of the uterus lengthen and the walls expand. A month before the bitch is due to whelp, incorporate fresh liver in her diet two or three times a week. This helps to keep her free from constipation and aids in the coming, necessary production of milk for the litter. If the litter is going to be small, she will not show much sign until late in the gestation period. But if the litter is going to be a normal or large one, she will begin to show distention of the abdomen at about thirty-five days after the breeding. Her appetite will have been increasing during this time, and gradually the fact of her pregnancy will become more and more evident.

THE WHELPING BOX

Several days before she is due to whelp, the whelping box should be prepared. It should be located in a dimly lit area removed from disturbance by other dogs, or humans. The box should be 30″ square, enclosed on all sides by eight- to ten-inch high boards, either plank or plywood. Boards must be added above these in about three weeks to keep the pups from climbing out. Three inches up from the flooring (when it is packed down), a half by two-inch smooth wooden slat should be attached to the sides with small angle irons, all around as a rail, or a pipe rail can be used. This will prevent the bitch from accidentally squeezing to death any puppy which crawls behind her. On the floor of the box lay a smooth piece of rubber matting which is easily removed and cleaned when the bedding is cleaned or changed. The bedding itself should be of rye or oat straw, and enough of it supplied so that the bitch can hollow out a nest and still leave some of the nesting material under the pups. Another method much used is to have several layers of newspapers in the bottom of the box so that they can be removed one or two at a time as they become soiled during whelping. After the litter is completely whelped, the straw bedding is provided and hollowed into a saucer shape so the whelps will be kept together in a limited area. The whelping box should be raised from the ground and a smaller box, or step provided, to make it easier for the bitch to enter or leave.

WHELPING THE LITTER

As the time approaches for the whelping, the bitch will become restless;

WHELPING BOX

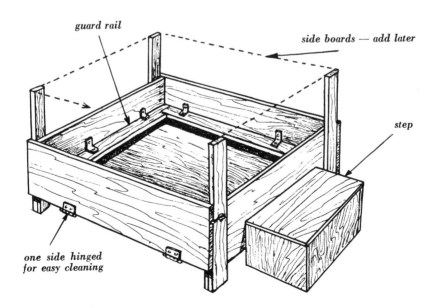

guard rail

side boards — add later

step

one side hinged
for easy cleaning

she may refuse food and begin to make her nest. Her temperature will drop approximately one degree the day before she is ready to whelp, and she will show a definite dropping down through the abdomen. Labor begins with pressure from within that forces the puppies toward the pelvis. The bitch generally twists around as the puppy is being expelled to lick the fluid which accompanies the birth. Sometimes the sac surrounding the puppy will burst from pressure. If it doesn't, the puppy will be born in the sac, a thin, membranous material called the fetal envelope. The navel cord runs from the

Most Cocker bitches are well able to take care of their own whelping and will look after the resulting litter with quiet efficiency, if all the circumstances surrounding the whelping are normal.

puppy's navel to the afterbirth, or placenta. If the bitch is left alone at whelping time, she will rip the fetal caul, bite off the navel cord and eat the sac, cord, and placenta. Should the cord be broken off in birth so that the placenta remains in the bitch, it will generally be expelled with the birth of the next whelp. After disposing of these items, the bitch will lick and clean the new puppy until the next one is about to be born, and the process will then repeat itself. Under completely normal circumstances, your bitch is quite able to whelp her litter and look after them without any help from you, but since the whelping might not be normal, it is best for the breeder to be present, particularly so in the case of bitches who are having their first litter.

The famous, Ch. My Own Brucie, in his day one of the greatest winners in the breed.

Below: Stockdale Stormalong, a fine show and stud dog of the past.

If the breeder is present, he or she can remove the sac, cut the umbilical cord, and gently pull on the rest of the cord, assuming that the placenta has not yet been ejected, until it is detached and drawn out. Some breeders keep a small box handy in which they place each placenta, so they can, when the whelping is completed, check them against the number of puppies to make sure that no placenta has been retained. The navel cord should be cut about three inches from the pup's belly. The surplus will dry up and drop off in a few days. There is no need to tie it after cutting. You need not attempt to sterilize your hands or the implements you might use in helping the bitch to whelp, since the pups will be practically surrounded with bacteria of all kinds, some benign and others which they are born equipped to combat.

If a bitch seems to be having difficulty in expelling a particularly large puppy, you can help by wrapping a towel around your hands to give you purchase, grasping the partly expelled whelp, and gently pulling. Do not pull too hard, or you might injure the pup. The puppies can be born either head first or tail first. Either way is normal. As the pups are born, the sac broken, and the cord snipped, dry them gently but vigorously with a towel

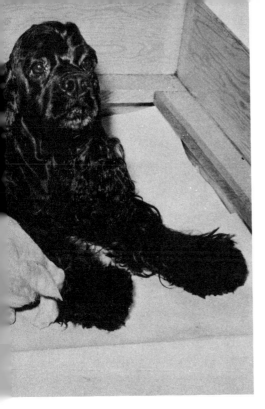

A bitch with her litter of puppies. This is the end result of the breeder's plans and dreams, the test of his skill and knowledge.

and put them at the mother's breast, first squeezing some milk to the surface and then opening their mouths for the entrance of the teat. You may have to hold them there by the head until they begin sucking.

Often several puppies are born in rapid succession, then an interval of time may elapse before another one is born. If the bitch is a slow whelper and seems to be laboring hard after one or more pups have been born, regular injections of Pitocin, at three-hour intervals, using about one-tenth c.c., can help her in delivery. Pituitrin, is a similar drug and the one most often used, though Pitocin brings less nausea and directly affects the uterus. Both these drugs should be administered hypodermically into the hind leg of the bitch at the rear of the thigh. After the bitch has seemingly completed her whelping, it is good practice to administer another shot of the drug to make sure no last pup, alive or dead, is still unborn and to cause her to clean out any residue left from the whelping. Never use either of these drugs until she has whelped at least one pup.

Allow her to rest quietly and enjoy the new sensation of motherhood for several hours, then insist that she leave her litter, though she won't want to,

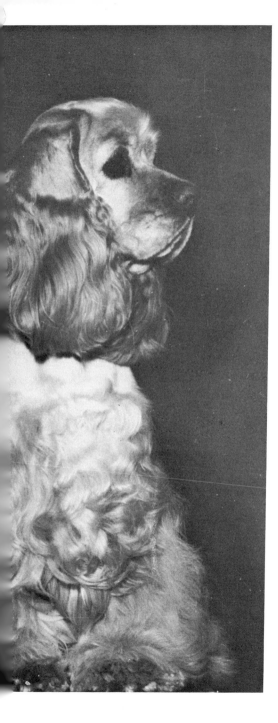

A lovely group of Abbis Cockers owned by Mrs. Harry Reno. Left to right they are: American and Canadian Ch. Abbis Adored Mister A.O.K., by Am. & Can. Ch. Darji's Abigail Lee x Can. Ch. Abbis Adorable Crumpet. In the middle is Abbis Mister A.O.K. and his litter sister, far right, Abbis Crumpet, at six months of age, both by, Ch. Jo-Be Glen's Bronze Falcon x Am. & Can. Ch. Darji's Abigail Lee.

and take her out to relieve herself. Offer her some warm milk. From then on, feed her as recommended during the gestation period, with the addition of three milk feedings per day. Sometimes milk appears in the udders before birth, but generally it comes in when the pups begin to nurse, since it is manufactured by glands, from blood, while the pups are at the breast.

Now is the time to cull the litter. Of course, all young which are not normal should be culled immediately at birth. If the bitch whelps six or less pups and all seem strong and healthy, no culling is required. If she has a particularly large litter, it does not pay, in the long run, to raise all the whelps. Allow her to keep five or six of the best and sturdiest and cull the rest. Those which you have retained will grow better and be larger and stronger than if you allowed the entire large litter to live. Quiet puppies are healthy ones. Constant crying and squirming of the pups is a danger signal, and a check should be made to see what ails them. It may be that the bitch is not providing enough milk and they are hungry, or perhaps they are cold. Sometimes the trouble is parasitic infection, or possibly coccidiosis, or navel infection. Dr. Walter Koch, in 1950, at the University of Munich, Animal Institute, reported a bacillus, Aerogenes, which he claimed caused many deaths of young puppies. This bacillus infects from contact with the dam's rectum. It multiplies rapidly in the whelp's intestines, and the normal bacillus in the stomach and intestines seems to have no effect on the lethal bacillus. It begins with the first digestion of the pups and attacks the basic internal organs, exhibiting symptoms on the second or third day following birth. The pups develop cramps, fail to suck, whimper, and die within two or three days. The disease does not seem to be contagious to other well puppies. If there is something wrong with the pups, whatever it may be, you need professional advice and should call your veterinarian immediately.

Except for the removal of dew claws and tail docking at five days, the pups, if healthy, need not be bothered until it is time to begin their supplementary feeding at about three weeks. Dew claws should be removed on about the second day after birth. Puppies and their needs, dietary and otherwise, are discussed more fully in another chapter.

There are several ills which might befall the bitch during gestation and whelping which must be considered. Eclampsia, sometimes called milk fever, is perhaps most common. This is a metabolic disturbance brought on by a deficiency of calcium and phosphorus in the diet. If you give your bitch plenty of milk and a good diet such as we have recommended, she should not be troubled with this condition. Should your bitch develop eclampsia—evidenced by troubled shaking, wild expression, muscular rigidity, and a high temperature—it can be quickly relieved by an injection of calcium gluconate in the vein.

Should your bitch be bred by accident to an undesirable animal, your

Ch. Hacker's Golden Challenge, a good red dog of the past.

Ch. Gilfran's Glider

Ch. Hodge's Honey Cloud, one of the fine, early parti-colored Cockers.

115

A lovely portrait photo of a top-winning Cocker in its day, Ch. Blair-wood Broom-Straw. This animal exhibits his notable head to perfection in this picture.

veterinarian can cause her to abort by the use of any one of several efficient canine abortifacients. He can also aid old bitches who have been resorbing their fetuses to carry them full term and whelp with the aid of stilbestrol.

Mastitis, an udder infection, is a chief cause of puppy deaths. It is generally mistaken by the uninformed for "acid milk," a condition which does not exist in dogs because the bitch's milk is naturally acid. Mastitis is an udder infection which cuts off part of the milk supply and the whelps either die of infection, contracted from the infected milk, or from starvation, due to the lack of sufficient milk. It is not necessary to massage the dam's breasts at weaning time with camphorated oil. They will cake naturally and quickly quit secreting milk if left completely alone.

Growths, infections, injuries, cysts, and other and various ailments can affect the female reproductive system and must be taken care of by your veterinarian. The great majority of bitches who have been well cared for and well fed are strong and healthy, and the bearing of litters is a natural procedure—the normal function of the female of the species to bear and rear the next generation, and in so doing fulfill her precious destiny.

Perpetual Whelping Chart

Bred—Jan. 1 2 3 4 5 6 7 8 9 10 11 12 13 14 15 16 17 18 19 20 21 22 23 24 25 26 27 28 29 30 31
Due—March 5 6 7 8 9 10 11 12 13 14 15 16 17 18 19 20 21 22 23 24 25 26 27 28 29 30 31 *April* 1 2 3 4

Bred—Feb. 1 2 3 4 5 6 7 8 9 10 11 12 13 14 15 16 17 18 19 20 21 22 23 24 25 26 27 28
Due—April 5 6 7 8 9 10 11 12 13 14 15 16 17 18 19 20 21 22 23 24 25 26 27 28 29 30 *May* 1 2

Bred—Mar. 1 2 3 4 5 6 7 8 9 10 11 12 13 14 15 16 17 18 19 20 21 22 23 24 25 26 27 28 29 30 31
Due—May 3 4 5 6 7 8 9 10 11 12 13 14 15 16 17 18 19 20 21 22 23 24 25 26 27 28 29 30 31 *June* 1 2

Bred—Apr. 1 2 3 4 5 6 7 8 9 10 11 12 13 14 15 16 17 18 19 20 21 22 23 24 25 26 27 28 29 30
Due—June 3 4 5 6 7 8 9 10 11 12 13 14 15 16 17 18 19 20 21 22 23 24 25 26 27 28 29 30 *July* 1 2

Bred—May 1 2 3 4 5 6 7 8 9 10 11 12 13 14 15 16 17 18 19 20 21 22 23 24 25 26 27 28 29 30 31
Due—July 3 4 5 6 7 8 9 10 11 12 13 14 15 16 17 18 19 20 21 22 23 24 25 26 27 28 29 30 31 *August* 1 2

Bred—June 1 2 3 4 5 6 7 8 9 10 11 12 13 14 15 16 17 18 19 20 21 22 23 24 25 26 27 28 29 30
Due—August 3 4 5 6 7 8 9 10 11 12 13 14 15 16 17 18 19 20 21 22 23 24 25 26 27 28 29 30 *Sept.* 1 2

Bred—July 1 2 3 4 5 6 7 8 9 10 11 12 13 14 15 16 17 18 19 20 21 22 23 24 25 26 27 28 29 30 31
Due—September 2 3 4 5 6 7 8 9 10 11 12 13 14 15 16 17 18 19 20 21 22 23 24 25 26 27 28 29 30 *Oct.* 1 2

Bred—Aug. 1 2 3 4 5 6 7 8 9 10 11 12 13 14 15 16 17 18 19 20 21 22 23 24 25 26 27 28 29 30 31
Due—October 3 4 5 6 7 8 9 10 11 12 13 14 15 16 17 18 19 20 21 22 23 24 25 26 27 28 29 30 31 *Nov.* 1 2

Bred—Sept. 1 2 3 4 5 6 7 8 9 10 11 12 13 14 15 16 17 18 19 20 21 22 23 24 25 26 27 28 29 30
Due—November 3 4 5 6 7 8 9 10 11 12 13 14 15 16 17 18 19 20 21 22 23 24 25 26 27 28 29 30 *Dec.* 1 2

Bred—Oct. 1 2 3 4 5 6 7 8 9 10 11 12 13 14 15 16 17 18 19 20 21 22 23 24 25 26 27 28 29 30 31
Due—December 3 4 5 6 7 8 9 10 11 12 13 14 15 16 17 18 19 20 21 22 23 24 25 26 27 28 29 30 31 *Jan.* 1 2

Bred—Nov. 1 2 3 4 5 6 7 8 9 10 11 12 13 14 15 16 17 18 19 20 21 22 23 24 25 26 27 28 29 30
Due—January 3 4 5 6 7 8 9 10 11 12 13 14 15 16 17 18 19 20 21 22 23 24 25 26 27 28 29 30 31 *Feb.* 1

Bred—Dec. 1 2 3 4 5 6 7 8 9 10 11 12 13 14 15 16 17 18 19 20 21 22 23 24 25 26 27 28 29 30 31
Due—February 2 3 4 5 6 7 8 9 10 11 12 13 14 15 16 17 18 19 20 21 22 23 24 25 26 27 28 *March* 1 2 3 4

The good stud dog need not necessarily be a champion or a big winner, but he must be typical of the breed and a proven producer of excellent puppies. This, the production of fine young, is the only measure of a stud dog's worth.

VIII

The Stud Dog

If what we have said about the unrivaled importance of the brood bitch is true, it may be difficult to understand why we pay so much attention to the male lines of descent. The reason is that stud dogs tend to mold the aspects of the breed on the whole and in any given locality, to a much greater extent than do brood bitches. While the brood bitch may control type in a kennel, the stud dog can control type over a much larger area. The truth of this can be ascertained by the application of simple mathematics.

Let us assume that the average litter is comprised of five puppies. The brood bitch will produce, then, a maximum of ten puppies a year. In that same year a popular, good producing, well-publicized stud dog may be used on the average of three times weekly (many name studs, in various breeds, have been used even more frequently over a period of several years). This popular stud can sire fifteen puppies a week, employing the figures mentioned above, or 780 puppies a year. Compare this total to the bitch's yearly total of ten puppies, and you can readily see why any one stud dog wields a much greater influence over the breed in general than does a specific brood bitch.

GENERAL CARE OF THE STUD DOG

The care of the stud dog follows the same procedure as outlined in the chapter on general care. He needs a balanced diet, clean quarters, and plenty of exercise, but no special care as does the brood bitch. Though it is against most of the advice previously written on the subject, we recommend that the stud be used in breeding for the first time when he is about twelve months old. He is as capable of siring a litter of fine and healthy pups at this age as he ever will be. He should be bred to a steady, knowing bitch who has been bred before, and when she is entirely ready to accept him. Aid him if necessary this first time. See that nothing disturbs him during copulation. In fact, the object of this initial breeding is to see that all goes smoothly and easily.

119

If you succeed in this aim, the young dog will be a willing and eager stud for the rest of his life, the kind of stud that it is a pleasure to own and use.

After this first breeding, use him sparingly until he has reached sixteen or seventeen months of age. After that, if he is in good health, there is no reason why he cannot be used at least twice a week or more during his best and most fertile years.

MALE REPRODUCTIVE ORGANS

The male organs vital for reproduction consist of a pair each of: testicles, where the sperm is produced; epididymis, in which the sperm are stored; and *vas deferens*, through which the sperm are transported. The dog possesses no seminal vesicle as does man. But, like man, the male dog is always in an active stage of reproduction and can be used at any time.

MECHANICS OF MATING

When the stud has played with the bitch for a short period and the bitch is ready, he will cover her. There is a bone in his penis, and behind this bone is a group of very sensitive nerves which cause a violent thrust reflex when pressure is applied. His penis, unlike most other animals', has a bulbous enlargement at its base. When the penis is thrust into the bitch's vagina, it goes through a muscular ring at the opening of the vagina. As it passes into the vagina, pressure on the reflex nerves causes a violent thrust forward, and the penis, and particularly the bulb, swells enormously, preventing withdrawal through the constriction band of the vulva. The stud ejaculates semen swarming with sperm, which is forced through the cervix, uterus, Fallopian tubes, and into the capsule which surrounds the ovaries, and the breeding is consummated.

The dog and bitch are tied, or "hung," and the active part of the breeding is completed. The owner of the bitch should then stand at her head and hold her by the collar. The stud's owner should kneel next to the animals with his arm or knee under the bitch's stomach, directly in front of her hindquarters, to prevent her from suddenly sitting while still tied. He should talk soothingly to the stud and gently prevent him from attempting to leave the bitch for a little while. Presently the stud owner should turn the dog around off the bitch's back by first lifting the front legs off and to the ground and then lifting one hind leg over the back of the bitch until dog and bitch are standing tail to tail, or side by side if the stud prefers.

Dogs remain in this position for various lengths of time after copulation, but fifteen minutes to a half an hour is generally average. When the congestion of blood leaves the penis, the bulb shrinks and the animals part.

The stud dog owner should keep a muzzle handy to be used on snappy

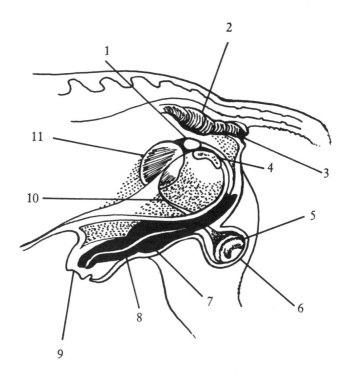

REPRODUCTIVE SYSTEM OF MALE

1. *Prostate* 2. *Rectum* 3. *Anus* 4. *Section of Pelvic bone* 5. *Testicle* 6. *Scrotum*
7. *Bulb (part of penis)* 8. *Penis* 9. *Sheath* 10. *Vas deferens* 11. *Bladder*

bitches. Many bitches, due to temperament, environment, or fright, may cause injury to the stud by biting. If she shows any indication of such conduct, she should be muzzled. Should she continue to attempt to bite for any length of time, it is generally because it is either too early or too late in the estrum cycle to consummate a breeding. If the bitch is small, sinks down when mounted, or won't stand, she must be held up. In some instances her owner or the stud's owner will have to kneel next to her and, with his hand under and between her hind legs, push the vulva up toward the dog's penis or guide the stud's penis into her vulva. Straw or earth, pushed under her hind legs to elevate her rear quarters, is effective in the case of a bitch who is very much too small for the stud.

As mentioned before, many novice bitch owners fail to recognize the initial signs of the oncoming heat period, or neglect to check, so that their knowledge of elapsed time since the first showing of red is only approximate. Many offer little aid in the attempt to complete the breeding, and talk incessantly and to no purpose, generally expressing wonder at their bitch's

A proud father and his son. The stud is Begay's St. Nick, by Ch. Hallway Hoot Mon x Merikays War Bonnet, C.D. The youngster is Begays Con Man of Condoro. Both sire and son owned and bred by Bill Ernst.

123

unorthodox conduct, but do little to quiet her. In many instances, particularly with a novice of the opposite sex, these actions are due to embarrassment. Regardless of the reason, remember to use the muzzle only on the bitch. We must always put the welfare of our dogs ahead of self.

MANAGING A STUD

There is not much more that can be written about the stud, except to caution the stud owner to be careful of using drugs or injections to make his dog eager to mate or more fertile. The number of puppies born in any litter is not dependent upon the healthy and fertile male's sperm, but upon the number of eggs the bitch gives off. Should your dog prove sterile, look for basic causes first. If there seems to be no physical reason for his sterility, then a series of injections by your veterinarian (perhaps of A-P-L, anterior-pituitary-like injections) might prove efficacious.

It is often a good idea to feed the dog a light meal before he is used, particularly if he is a reluctant stud. Young, or virgin, studs often regurgitate due to excitement, but it does them no harm. After the tie has broken, allow both dog and bitch to drink moderately.

How often a stud dog should be used is a moot question. Earlier in this chapter I wrote, ". . . there is no reason why he cannot be used at least twice a week or more during his best and most fertile years." Twice a week seems little enough when we consider the fact that Red Brucie was bred to seven bitches the week before he died. I think we can truthfully say of this great dog that "he died happy". Consider also the fact that Brucie sired the famous "big four" litter when he was about a year old.

Ch. My Own Personality, bred by H. E. Mellenthin and owned by Mrs. C. Gillette.
sire: Ch. My Own Again
dam: My Own Joy

*Ch. Sleepy Hollow Sovereign, Best Black Sweep-
stakes, Cocker Spaniel Club of Kentucky, 1967,
under judge, Everett Dean. This splendid black
is handled by Ted Young, Jr., and is owned
by Mrs. Violet Myshrall.*

Many other famous sires in other breeds as well as in the Cocker breed have been, at the height of their popularity as studs, bred several times a week. It is the author's opinion that a strong, healthy stud dog between the ages of three and eight years can be used every other day with a week off every month.

I have known breeders, that small handful of the very lucky ones to have owned or bred a great stud dog, to have averaged over a long period of fertile years, a very fine yearly income from the stud efforts of their animal.

An eight weeks old puppy, now a champion. The pup is Champel's Sumpin' Flashy owned and bred by Elizabeth H. Ahrens.
sire: Ch. Valli-Lo's Flash A'Way
dam: Champel's Certainly Sumpin'

IX

Your Cocker Puppy

The birth of a litter has been covered in a previous chapter on the brood bitch. As we indicated in that discussion, barring accident or complications at birth, there is little you can do for your puppies until they are approximately three weeks old. At that age supplementary feedings begin. But suppose that for one reason or another the mother must be taken from her brood: What care must be given to these small Cockers if they are to survive? Puppies need warmth. This is provided partly by their instinctive habit of gathering together in the nest, but to a much greater extent by the warmth of the mother's body. If the mother must be taken from the nest, this extra warmth can be provided by an ordinary light bulb, or, better still, an infra-red bulb, hung directly over the brood in the enclosed nest box.

CARE OF NEWBORNS

By far the most important requirement of these newborn pups is proper food. Puppies are belly and instinct, and nothing much more. They must be fed well and frequently. What shall we feed them, what formula can we arrive at that most closely approaches the natural milk of the mother, which we know is best? There are prepared modified milks for orphan puppies which are commercially available and very worth while, or you can mix your own formula of ingredients which will most closely simulate natural bitch's milk. To do this, you must first know the basic quality of the dam's milk. Bitches' milk is comparatively acid; it contains less sugar and water, more ash and protein, and far more fat than cow or human milk, so we must modify our formula to conform to these differences.

To begin, purchase a can of Nestlé's Pelargon, a spray-dried, acidified, and homogenized modified milk product. If you can't get Pelargon, try any of the spray-dried baby milks, but Pelargon is best since it is, like bitches'

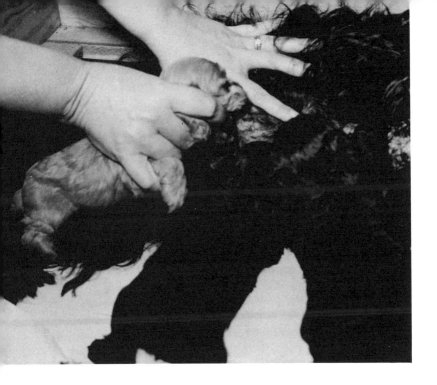

Putting the puppy on the mother's breast, sometimes necessary when the puppy is smaller than its litter mates and is being pushed away from its food supply.

milk, slightly acid and rich in necessary nutritive substances. To one ounce of the modified milk product, add one ounce of fresh cream. Pour six ounces of water by volume into this mixture and blend with an electric mixer or egg beater until it is smooth. Larger amounts can be mixed employing the same basic proportions and kept refrigerated. This formula should be fed five or six times a day and, when fed, must be warmed to body heat. Many puppies refuse to drink a formula which has not been warmed to just the right temperature.* Do not add lime water, glucose, or dextrose to the formula, for by so doing you are modifying in the wrong direction. An ordinary baby's bottle and nipple are adequate as the formula vehicle. Never drop liquids directly in the puppy's throat with an eye dropper or you invite pneumonia. A six ounce puppy will absorb one half ounce of formula, a twelve ounce puppy one ounce at each feeding A valuable adjunct to the

* Warm goat's milk is also excellent for cocker puppies.

128

puppy's diet, whether formula or breast fed, is two drops of Dietol, dropped into the lip pocket from the first day of birth on, the amount to be increased with greater growth and age. A bottle trough can be built for orphan pups. The trick here is to space the nipple holes so that the bodies of the pups touch when drinking.

If it is possible to find a foster mother for orphan pups, your troubles are over. Most lactating bitches will readily take to puppies other than their own if the new babies are first prepared by spreading some of the foster mother's milk over their tiny bodies. The foster mother will lick them clean and welcome them to the nest.

Dewclaws should be clipped off with a manicure scissors the day after birth, and when the puppies are five or six days old dock the tails (or have your veterinarian do it) where they begin to thin out, approximately the junction of the proximal and middle third. If done properly no stitches will be necessary.

A nice litter of Cocker puppies with tails already docked. Note the rail inside the whelping box whch can keep a valuable, newly born puppy from being crushed by a careless dam.

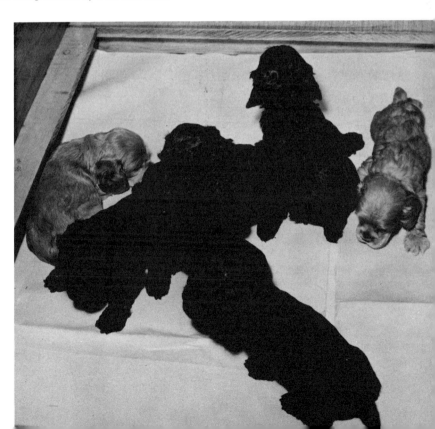

WEANING

When the puppies are two-and-a-half to three weeks old the dam will often engage in an action that is disgusting to the neophyte, but which is an instinctive and natural performance to the bitch. She will regurgitate her own stomach contents of partially digested food for her puppies to eat, thus beginning, in her own way, the weaning process. If you have begun supplementary feeding in time, this action by the bitch will seldom occur. If you haven't, it is a definite indication that supplementary feeding should begin at once.

Puppies grow best on milk, meat, fat, and cereal diets. Growth is attained through proteins, but proteins differ, so that puppies fed on vegetable protein diets will not grow and thrive as well as those fed animal proteins. Vitamins E and K (found in alfalfa meal) are essential to the pups' well being and should be used in adequate amounts in the food ration. Remember that 70 per cent of the pup's energy is derived from fat intake, so supply this food element generously in the diet. Lime water should not be incorporated in the diet since it neutralizes stomach acidity, a condition which is necessary to the assimilation of fat. In experiments, puppies on fat-free diets developed deficiency symptoms characterized by anemia, weight loss, dull coats, and finally, death. Fat alone could not cure the advanced manifestation of the condition, indicating that some metabolic process was disturbed when complete fat removal in the diet was resorted to. But feeding butterfat plus folacin resulted in dramatic cures.

To begin the small puppy on supplementary feeding, place the pan of food before him, gently grasp his head behind the ears, and dip his lips and chin into the food. The puppy will lick his lips, taste the food, and in no time at all learn to feed by himself. Be careful not to push the head in so far that the pup's nose is covered and clogged by food.

Check the puppies' navels every day to see that infection has not set in. This infection comes from the scraping of their soft bellies on a rough surface and can generally be avoided if several thicknesses of cloth covers the floor of the nest box under the bedding.

Clip the sharp little nails to avoid damage to litter mates' eyes, which will open at about ten days. Have a fecal check made when the pups are about three-and-a-half weeks old. If they are infested with worms, worm them immediately. Do not attempt to build up the pups first if the parasitic infestation has made them unthrifty. It is best to rid them of the worms quickly, after which they will speedily return to normal health and plumpness.

The weeks fly by, and before you know it the puppies are at saleable age. The breeder, you can be sure, has not wasted these weeks. He has spent many hours in close observation of the litter and has centered his interest

Teaching the puppy to drink warm milk from a
shallow pan is the first step in the weaning
process. After being shown once how to lap up the
milk most puppies need no more urging.

The top sporting dog winner of 1965, the grand
silver buff dog, Ch. Biggs Snow Prince, shown
here being handled to a group win at Harbor
Cities Kennel Club, by Ted Young, Jr. under
judge Alva Rosenberg. Prince is owned by
Mrs. H. Terrell Van Ingen.

on one pup which he thinks shows the most promise. Either he will hold this pup for himself, sell him to a show-conscious buyer, or keep the puppy and sell it at a higher price when it has become more fully developed and its early promise becomes a fact. The strange part about this whole business of picking a young puppy from a litter is that the novice buyer many times stands as good a chance of picking the best pup as the seasoned and experienced breeder. The reason for this seeming incongruity lies in the fact that in every litter there will be several pups which, if well bred and well cared for, appear to be potential winners at eight to ten weeks of age. Another reason concerns the ratio of sectional growth in young animals. Each pup, as an individual, will have a different growth rate and exhibit change in relative sections of the body, as well as in over-all growth, from day to day.

BUYING A PUPPY

If you are the potential purchaser of a Cocker puppy, or a grown dog for that matter, prepare yourself for the purchase first by attending as many shows as possible, especially shows where known Cocker specialty judges are officiating. Observe, absorb, and listen. Visit kennels which have well-bred, winning stock, and at shows and kennels make an unholy nuisance of yourself by asking innumerable questions of people who have proved, by their record in the breed, that information gleaned from them can be respected. When you intend to purchase a new car, or an electrical appliance such as a refrigerator or washing machine, you go to sales rooms and examine the different makes, weighing their features and quality, one against the other. You inquire of friends who have different brands their opinion in regard to the utility value of the item, and, when you have made your up mind which brand is best, you make sure that you purchase the item from a reliable distributor. Do the same thing when you intend to purchase a dog. Before you make your journey to any breeder to buy a puppy, be sure to inquire first into the background of the breeder as well as the background of his dogs. What does this breeder actually know about his breed? What has he formerly produced? What is his reputation amongst other reputable breeders? Does his stock have balanced minds as well as balanced bodies? Find the answers to these questions even before you delve into the ancestry of the puppies he has for sale. If the answers prove that this breeder is an honest, dependable person with more than a smattering knowledge of the breed, and that he has bred consistently typical stock, then your next step will be to study the breeding of his puppies to determine whether they have been bred from worth-whiie stock which comes from good producing strains. Examine stock he has sold from different breedings to other customers. Be careful of kennels which are puppy factories, breeding solely for commercial reasons, and don't be carried away by hysterical, overdone, adjective-happy advertisements.

When you have satisfied yourself that the breeder is a morally responsible person who has good stock, then you may sally forth to purchase your future champion. It is best, if possible, to invite an experienced breeder to accompany you on your mission. As mentioned before, even the most experienced cannot with assurance pick the pup in the litter which will mature into the best specimen. An experienced person can, however, keep you from selecting a very engaging youngster which exhibits obvious faults which quite possibly won't improve.

Assuming that the litter from which you are going to select your puppy is a fat and healthy one and it is a male puppy you have set your heart on having, ask the breeder to separate the sexes so you can examine the male pups only. Normal puppies are friendly, lovable creatures wanting immediate attention, so the little fellow who backs away from you and runs away and hides should be eliminated from consideration immediately. This

A pair of nice pups owned by Elizabeth H. Ahrens. These youngsters are eight weeks old in this photo, and were named Champel's Flashy Flipper (call name, "Flip") and Champel's Flashy Lassie (call name, "Dolly"). Parents of the pups are, Ch. Valli-Lo's Flash A'Way and Champel's Certainly Sumpin'.

The sign tells the story of this impressive win made by the beautiful red dog Ch. Eufaula's Dividend, 1956. Ted Young, Jr., is the handler, Norman A. Austin the judge, and the proud owner is Mr. C. E. Dimon.

also applies to the pup which sulks in a corner and wants no part of the proceedings. Watch the puppies from a distance of approximately twenty feet as they play and frolic, sometimes trotting and occasionally quitting their play for a fleeting moment to stand gazing at something of interest which has, for that second, engaged their attention. Don't be rushed. Take all the time necessary to pick the puppy you want. You are about to pay cold cash for a companion who will be with you for many years.

If you have been lucky enough to have had the opportunity of examining both sire and dam (or hunted behind them), determine which puppies exhibit the faults of the parents or the strain. If any particular fault seems to be overdone in a specific pup, discard him from further consideration. Do not handle the pups during this preliminary examination. Look for over-all balance first and the absence of glaring structural faults, but remember that the good pup will show an exaggeration of all the excellencies you expect to be present in the mature animal. Shy or frightened puppies (and grown dogs) have a tendency to crouch a bit, giving the illusion of beautiful hindquarter angulation, where the bold dog, who possesses equal angulation will appear straighter behind. Watch the pup's movement when at a trot. A good one moves with a balanced, though ungainly, trot. Look particularly for a long reach in front, which indicates good shoulder angulation. Hindquarters often improve, except when the hock is straight and angulation is sorely lacking at this age, but front assemblies seldom change. A dog with good shoulders and reach can be depended upon to get the most from what he has when moving. Angulation, fore and aft, should be determined without handling, since a pup has a tendency to crouch when set up for examination, exaggerating the angle of skeletal structure in these sections. The importance of the shoulder should be remembered by the novice, since the eye is usually first engaged by exaggerated rear angulation.

If you are selecting a puppy for possible showing later, look for a good square-cut muzzle, a sharp and deep stop, and a clean skull not too wide for the muzzle. The head should appear blocky but not coarse, the ears set low on the skull. The nasal line, in profile, should be straight, and the nose good

When you purchase a puppy be sure that you receive its A.K.C. registration paper, a three generation pedigree, and a record of wormings, shots, etc., in short a medical history.

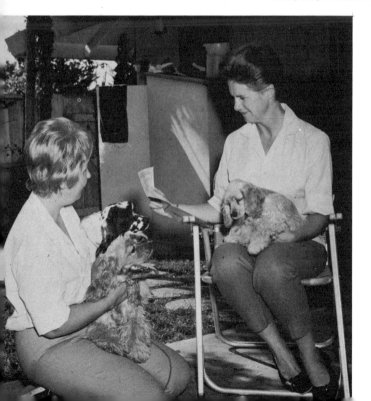

sized. The eyes should be round and full and exhibit lively intelligence. Select for a long ("reachy") dry neck rising from clean, well-angulated shoulders. The body should be square, sturdy, the back straight, strong, and sloping gently toward the tail. Legs should be well-boned, short in pastern strongly angulated in hindquarters. A solid color would probably be your best bet for showing.

For a gun or field dog, select an animal that is well up to size with good legs and feet, thick tough footpads, deep in the jaw, strong all over and showing exceptional willingness, intelligence and staunchness to sound. A parti-colored dog is more easily seen in the field than a solid color.

In each instance, whether for show or field, select a puppy whose ancestry indicates that he was bred for your purpose.

If you desire only a pet, look for intelligence, willingness, sweetness, good health and generally good Cocker type, color optional.

Female puppies are generally slightly smaller and show a degree of greater refinement than the males.

Remember that no one can pick a champion at eight weeks and no breeder can truthfully sell you a future winner at that age. All a breeder can guarantee is the health and breeding of the puppy, and the fact that he possesses the normal complement of eyes, ears and legs. The best you can do if you are observant, knowing, and lucky, is to pick the best pup in that particular litter, at that particular time.

THE PUPPY IN A NEW HOME

If it is at all possible, it is best to purchase two pups at the same time. They furnish company for each other, eliminate lonesome serenades during the first few nights, and are competition at the food pan. If you bring home only one pup, provide him with a stuffed dog or doll in his sleeping box which you have taken to the breeder's with you and rubbed in the nest box. This will frequently give the puppy some sense of comfort and companionship and alleviate lonesomeness that brings on dismal howling during the first night in his new home. A ticking alarm clock near the pup's bed will sometimes have the same effect.

In his new home, amidst strange surroundings, the pup will very often go off his feed for a time. This should not unduly alarm you unless his refusal to eat lasts so long that he becomes emaciated. If this occurs, ask your veterinarian for a good tonic, or change diets to tempt his palate. Never coax him or resort to forced feeding, or you will immediately spoil your pup and be a slave to him and his aggravating eating habits from that time forward. If he eats only one or two meals a day, instead of the several feedings he should have, he will survive until his appetite improves if he is otherwise

Lovely, well bred, show type puppies, well groomed and healthy, the kind that both seller and buyer can be proud of. Quality is evident in these youngsters, and the buyer must be prepared to pay a decent price for such stock.

Ch. Hugomar Headliner, owned by Mr. Albert W. Siekierski, is shown adding to his exceptional record with a group first at the Fort Lauderdale Kennel Club under judge James W. Trullinger, handler Ted Young, Jr. This dog was the top-winning tricolor Cocker in the United States during 1967.

healthy and vigorous. Should you find after a reasonable time and much scheming and effort that you have a naturally finicky eater, you must resign yourself to the fact that you have acquired a headache which can last for the duration of your dog's life and one which cannot be cured by aspirin. Only heroic measures can help you conquer this difficulty, and you must steel yourself and cast out pity if you are to succeed. He must be starved, but really starved, until he has reached a point where dry bread resembles the most succulent beef. Only by such drastic measures can a finicky eater be cured. Dogs who have the competition of other dogs, or even a cat, at the feed pan usually display a normal appetite. For this reason it is sometimes smart for the one-dog owner to borrow a friend's or neighbor's pet to feed with his own until such time as his own dog has acquired a healthful and adequate appetite.

Arrange for your pup to have lots of sleep, particularly after feeding, a difficult chore when there are youngsters in the home, but nevertheless very necessary to the well being of the pup. Make him feel at home so he will respond quickly to his new surroundings. It so often happens that a puppy retained by the breeder surpasses at maturity the purchased pup who was a better specimen in the beginning. This confounds the novice, yet has a reasonably simple explanation. The retained pup had no change in environment which would effect his appetite and well being during the critical period of growth, while the bought pup had and so was outstripped by his lesser litter brother.

Your puppy will have two sets of teeth, the milk teeth, which will have fallen out by the time he is approximately six months of age, and the permanent teeth, which he'll retain for the rest of his life. Loss of weight and fever may accompany the eruption of the new, permanent teeth, but is no cause for alarm. Anatomists have a simple formula to represent the number and arrangement of permanent teeth which, at a glance, will allow you to determine if your dog has his full complement of teeth, and if he hasn't, which ones are missing. In the chart below, the horizontal line represents the division between upper and lower jaw. We begin with the incisors in the front of the dog's mouth and designate them with the letter *I*. The canine teeth are labeled *C*, the premolars, *P*, and the molars, *M*. The complete formula for a dog possessing all his teeth would be:

$$I\,\frac{3+3}{3+3}+C\,\frac{1+1}{1+1}+P\,\frac{4+4}{4+4}+M\,\frac{2+2}{3+3}=42 \text{ teeth}$$

(20 in upper jaw)
(22 in lower jaw)

The correct scissors bite.

Occasionally, puppies develop lip warts which will disappear in a short time, leaving no aftereffects. Remember to have your puppy immunized against distemper and hepatitis and, as much as possible, keep him away from other dogs until he is old enough to combat the diseases which take their toll of the very young. Lastly, but of great importance, give your pup the opportunity to develop that character and intelligence for which the Cocker Spaniel is justly famed. Give him human companionship and understanding, take him with you in the car and amongst strangers. Let him live the normal, happy, and useful life which is his heritage, and that tiny bundle of fur which you brought home so short a time ago will grow into a canine citizen of whom you will be proud to say, "He's mine."

141

The Cocker Spaniel, with its heritage of field work for man, lends itself, as a breed, to all kinds of training. Many Cockers, not shown or used in the field, bring great pleasure to their owners through obedience trial competition.

X

Fundamental Training for the Cocker Spaniel

Responsibility for the reputation of any breed is shared by everyone who owns a specimen of that breed. Reputation, good or bad, is achieved by conduct, and conduct is the result of the molding, through training, of inherent character into specific channels of behavior.

It is a distinct pleasure, to novice, old-timer, or the public at large, to watch dogs perform which have been trained to special tasks. Here is the ultimate, the end result of the relationship between man and dog. After watching an inspired demonstration, we sometimes wonder if, under a proper training regime, our own dog could do as well. Perhaps he can if he is temperamentally fitted for the task we have in mind. No single individual of any breed, regardless of breed type, temperament, and inheritance, is fitted to cope with all the branches of specialized service. Nor does every owner possess the qualifications or experience necessary to train dogs successfully to arduous tasks. But every dog can be trained in the fundamentals of decent behavior, and every dog owner can give his dog this basic training. It is, indeed, the duty of every dog owner to teach his dog obedience to command as well as the necessary fundamentals of training which insure good conduct and gentlemanly deportment. A dog that is uncontrolled can become a nuisance and even a menace. This dog brings grief to his owner and bad reputation to himself and the breed he represents.

We cannot attempt, in this limited space, to write a complete and comprehensive treatise on all the aspects of dog training. There are several worthwhile books, written by experienced trainers, that cover the entire varied field of initial and advanced training. There are, furthermore, hundreds of training classes throughout the country where both the dog and its owner receive standard obedience training for a nominal fee, under the guidance of experienced trainers. Here in these pages you will find only specific

143

*Owned by Mr. and Mrs. Wm.
Coppola and ably handled by Ted
Young, Jr., the handsome buff dog,
Ch. Kahola's Key Stone, is shown
here, in 1965, going Best Of
Variety at the American Spaniel
Club Zone I Show. The judge
is Leslie Wagner.*

suggestions on some points of simple basic training which we feel are neglected in most of the books on this subject. We will also attempt to give you basic reasons for training techniques and explain natural limitations to aid you in eliminating future, perhaps drastic, mistakes.

The key to all canine training, simple or advanced, is control. Once you have established control over your Cocker, you can, if you so desire, progress to advanced or specialized training in other fields. The dog's only boundaries to learning are his own basic limitations. This vital control must be established during the basic training in good manners.

Almost every Cocker is responsive to training. He loves his master and finds delight in pleasing him. To approach the training problem with your Cocker, to make it a pleasant and easy intimacy rather than an arduous and wearisome task, you must first learn a few fundamentals. In the preceding paragraph we spoke of control as the paramount essential in training. To gain control over your dog, you must first establish control over your own vagaries of temperament. During training, when you lose your temper, you lose control. Shouting, nagging repetition, angry reprimand, and exasperation only confuse your canine pupil. If he does not obey, then the lesson has not been learned. He needs teaching, not punishment. The time of training should be approached with pleasure by both master and dog, so that both you and your pupil look forward to these periods of contact. If you establish this atmosphere, your dog will enjoy working, and a dog who enjoys his work, who is constantly trying to please, is a dog who is always under control.

Consistency is the brother of control in training. Perform each movement used in schooling in the same manner every time. Use the same words of command or communication without variance. Employ command words that are simple, single syllables, chosen for their crispness and difference in sound. Don't call your dog to you one day with the command, "Come," and the next day, with the command, "Here," and expect the animal to understand and perform the act with alacrity. Inconsistency confuses your dog. If your are inconsistent, the dog will not perform correctly and your control is lost. By consistency you establish habit patterns which eventually become an inherent part of your Cocker's behavior. Remember that a few simple commands, well learned, are much better than many and varied commands only partially absorbed. Therefore be certain that your dog completely understands a command and will perform the action it demands, quickly and without hesitation, before attempting to teach him a new command.

Before we begin training, we must first assess our prospective pupil's intelligence and character. We must understand that his eyesight is not as keen as ours, but that he is quick to notice movement. We must know that

* For more detailed information on basic training see the author's book, How To Train Your Dog, published by TFH Publications, Inc.

Training the Cocker to submit to trimming and clipping can be accomplished at a very early age. If started young, as shown above, the pup soon becomes used to the sound and touch of the clippers and will show no fear of the equipment when the time comes to earnestly use it.

sound and scent are his chief means of communication with his world, and that in these departments he is far superior to us. We must reach him, then, through voice and gesture, and realize that he is very sensitive to quality change and intonation of the commanding voice. Therefore, any given command must have a definite tonal value in keeping with its purpose. The word "No" used in reprimand must be expressed sharply and with overtones of displeasure, while "Good boy," employed as praise, should be spoken lightly and pleasantly. In early training, the puppy recognizes distinctive sound coupled with the quality of tone used rather than individual words.

All words of positive command should be spoken sharply and distinctly during training. By this we do not mean that commands must be shouted, a practice which seems to be gaining favor in obedience work and which is very much to be deplored. A well-trained, mature Cocker can be kept completely under control and will obey quickly and willingly, when commands are given in an ordinary conversational tone. The first word a puppy

Paper-breaking the young Cocker puppy is an easy task because of the innate intelligence of the breed. Later it will not be difficult to teach your Cocker to use the outdoors.

learns is the word-sound of his name; therefore, in training, his name should be spoken first to attract his attention to the command which follows. Thus, when we want our dog to come to us, and his name is Bruce, we command, "Bruce! Come!"

Intelligence varies in dogs as it does in all animals, human or otherwise. The ability to learn and to perform is limited by intelligence, facets of character, and structure, such as willingness, energy, sensitivity, aggressiveness, stability, and functional ability. The sensitive dog must be handled with greater care and quietness in training than the less sensitive animal. Aggressive dogs must be trained with firmness; and an animal which possesses a structural fault which makes certain of the physical aspects of training a painful experience cannot be expected to perform these acts with enjoyment and consistency.

In referring to intelligence, we mean, of course, canine intelligence. Dogs are supposedly unable to reason, since that portion of the brain which, in humans, is the seat of the reasoning power is not highly developed in the dog. Yet there have been so many reported incidents of canine behavior that seemingly could not have been actuated by instinct, training, stored knowledge, or the survival factor, that we are led to wonder if the dog may not

148

possess some primitive capacity for reasoning which, in essence, is so different from the process of human reasoning that it has been overlooked, or is as yet beyond the scope of human comprehension.

Training begins the instant the puppies in the nest feel the touch of your hand and are able to hear the sound of your voice. Once the pup is old enough to run and play, handle him frequently, petting him, making a fuss over him, speaking in soothing and pleasant tones and repeating his name over and over again. When you bring him his meals, call him by name and coax him to "Come." As time passes, he associates the command "Come" with a pleasurable experience and will come immediately upon command. Every time he obeys a command, he should be praised or rewarded. When calling your puppies to their food, it is good practice to use some kind of distinguishing sound accompanying the command—a clucking or "beep" sound. It is amazing how this distinctive sound will be retained by the dog's memory, so that years after it has ceased to be used, he will still remember and respond to the sound.

LEAD TRAINING

Some professional trainers and handlers put soft collars on tiny pups, with

Feeding the Cocker youngster, a pleasurable experience for the pup, can be utilized by the trainer as the initial stage in conditioning the Cocker to obey commands, particularly the "Come!" command.

a few inches of thin rope attached to the collar clip. The puppies, in play, tug upon these dangling pieces of rope hanging from the collars of their litter mates, thus preparing the youngsters for easy leash breaking in the future. In training the pup to the leash, be sure to use a long leash, and coax, do not drag the reluctant puppy, keeping him always on your left side. Never use the leash as an implement of punishment.

HOUSEBREAKING

Housebreaking is usually the tragedy of the novice dog owner. We who have Cockers are fortunate in this respect since, as a breed, they are basically clean in habits and quite easily housebroken. Many Cockers which are raised outside in a run never need to be actually housebroken, preferring to use the ground for their act and seemingly sensing the fact that the house is not to be soiled. Dogs tend to defecate in areas which they, or other dogs, have previously soiled, and will go to these spots if given the chance. Directly after eating or waking a puppy almost inevitably has to relieve himself. If he is in the house and makes a mistake, it is generally your fault, as you should have recognized these facts and removed him in time to avert disaster. If, after you have taken him out, he comes in and soils the floor or rug, he must be made to realize that he has done wrong. Scold him with, "Shame! Shame!" and rush him outside. Praise him extravagantly when he has taken advantage of the great outdoors. Sometimes if you catch him preparing to void in the house, a quick, sharp, "No" will stop the proceedings and allow you time to usher him out. Never rub his nose in his excreta. Never indulge in the common practice of striking the puppy with a rolled up newspaper or with your hand. If you do, you may be training your dog either to be hand shy, to be shy of paper, or to bite the newsboy. Your hand should be used only in such a way that your dog recognizes it as that part of you which implements your voice, to pet and give pleasure. In housebreaking, a "No", or "Shame" appropriately used and delivered in an admonishing tone is punishment enough.

A working Cocker is seldom broken to paper in the house. If your dog has been so trained and subsequently you wish to train him to use the outdoors, a simple way to teach him this is to move the paper he has used outside, anchoring it with stones. Lead the dog to the paper when you know he is ready to void. Each day make the paper smaller until it has completely disappeared, and the pup will have formed the habit of going on the spot previously occupied by the paper. Puppies tend to prefer to void on a surface similar in texture to that which they used in their first few weeks of life. Thus a pup who has had access to an outside run is easily housebroken, preferring the feel of ground under him. Cockers are sometimes raised on wire-bottom pens to keep them free of intestinal parasites. Occasionally puppies so raised have been brought into homes with central heating employing an open grate-covered duct in the floor. To the pup the grate feels similar to his former wire-bottomed pen. The result, as you can well imagine, gives rise to much profanity and such diligence that the youngster is either rapidly housebroken or just as rapidly banished to live outdoors.

If your Cocker is to be a housedog, a lot of grief can be avoided by remembering a few simple rules. Until he is thoroughly clean in the house, confine him to one room at night, preferably a tile or linoleum-floored room that can be cleaned easily. Tie him so that he cannot get beyond the radius of his bed, or confine him to a dog house within the room; few dogs will soil their beds or sleeping quarters. Feed at regular hours and you will soon learn the interval between the meal and its natural result and take the pup out in time. Give water only after meals until he is housebroken. Puppies, like inveterate drunks, will drink constantly if the means is available, and there is no other place for surplus water to go but out. The result is odd puddles at odd times.

TRAINING FOR GOOD MANNERS

"No," "Shame," "Come," and "Good boy" (or "girl"), spoken in appropriate tones, are the basic communications you will use in initial training.

If your pup is running free and he doesn't heed your command to come, do not chase him—he will only run away or dodge your attempts to catch him and your control over him will be completely lost. Attract his attention by calling his name and, when he looks in your direction, turn and run away from him, calling him as you do so. In most instances he will quickly run after you. Even if it takes a great deal of time and much exasperation to get him to come to you, never scold him once he has. Praise him instead. *A puppy should only be scolded when he is caught in the act of doing something he shouldn't do.* If he is scolded even a few minutes after he has committed his error, he will not associate the punishment with the crime and will be bewildered and unhappy about the whole thing, losing his trust in you.

Puppies are inveterate thieves. It is natural for them to steal food from the table. The "No!" and "Shame!" command, or reprimand, should be used to correct this breach of manners. The same commands are employed when the pup uses your living room couch as a sleeping place. Many times dogs are aware that they must not sleep on the furniture, but are clever enough to avoid punishment by using the sofa only when you are out. They will hastily leave the soft comfort of the couch when they hear you approaching and greet you in wide-eyed innocence, models of canine virtue. Only the tell-tale hairs, the dent in the cushion, and the body heat on the fabric are

In 1954, Best In Show at the American Spaniel Club was the top black dog, Ch. Taylor's Dark Knight. Ted Young, Jr. is shown here handling Knight to this win under judge Clyde Heck. The fortunate owner of this fine dog is Dr. Gilbert H. Taylor.

clues to the culprit's dishonesty. This recalls the tale of the dog who went just a step further. So clever was he that when his master approached, he would leap from the couch and, standing before it, blow upon the cushions to dislodge the loose hairs and cool the cushion's surface. The hero of this tale of canine duplicity was not identified as to breed, but we are sure that such intelligence could only have been displayed by a Cocker.

If, like the dog in the story, the pup persists in committing this misdemeanor, we must resort to another method to cure him. Where before we used a positive approach, we must now employ a negative, and rather sneaky, method. The idea is to trick the pup into thinking that when he commits these crimes he punishes himself and that we have been attempting to stop him from bringing this punishment down upon his head. To accomplish this end with the unregenerate food thief, tie a tempting morsel of food to a long piece of string. To the string attach several empty tin cans, or small bells, eight to ten inches apart. Set the whole contraption on the kitchen or dining-room table, with the food morsel perched temptingly on an accessible edge. Leave the room and allow the little thief to commit his act of dishonesty. When you hear the resultant racket, rush into the room, sternly mouthing the appropriate words of reproach. You will generally find a thoroughly chastened pup who, after one or two such lessons, will eye any tabled food askance and leave it strictly alone.

The use of mousetraps is a neat little trick to cure the persistent sofa-hopper. Place two or three set traps on the couch area the dog prefers and cover them with a sheet of newspaper. When he jumps up on the sofa, he will spring the traps and leave that vicinity in a great and startled hurry.

These methods, or slight variations, can be used in teaching your pup to resist many youthful temptations such as dragging and biting rugs, furniture, tablecloths, draperies, curtains, etc.

The same approach, in essence, is useful in teaching the pup not to jump up on your friends and neighbors. You can lose innumerable friends if your mud-footed dog playfully jumps up on the visitor wearing a new suit or dress. If the "No" command alone does not break him of this habit, hold his front legs and feet tightly in your hands when he jumps up, and retain your hold. The pup finds himself in an uncomfortable and unnatural position standing on his hind legs alone. He will soon tug and pull to release his front legs from your hold. Retain your hold in the face of his struggles until he is heartily sick of the strained position he is in. A few such lessons and he will refrain from committing an act which brings such discomfort in its wake.

Remember that only by positive training methods can you gain control which is the basis of successful training, and these tricky methods do not give you that control. They are simply short-cut ways of quickly rectifying nuisance habits, but do nothing to establish the "rapport" which must exist between trainer and dog.

During the entire puppy period the basis is being laid for other and more advanced training. The acts of discipline, of everyday handling, grooming, and feeding, are preparation for the time when he is old enough to be taught the meaning of the Sit, Down, Heel, Stand, and Stay, commands which are the first steps in obedience training and commands which every dog should be taught to obey immediately. Once you have learned how to train your dog and have established complete control, further training is only limited by your own abilities and by the natural boundaries which exist within the animal himself.

Top right shows us a Cocker being instructed by his young mistress, in how to take the high jump . . . a little at a time.

Bottom right: The dog's mistress is indicating, with proper enthusiasm, her delight at her pupil's performance in obedience.

At left, this nice black Cocker is in a perfect "Sit" at his young master's side.

Don't rush your training. Be patient with small progress. Training for both you and your dog will become easier as you progress. Make sure that whatever you teach him is well and thoroughly learned, and it will never be forgotten. Remember to use simple common sense when you approach the task of training. Approach it with ease and confidence. Control yourself if you wish to control your dog, for control is the vital element in all training. Realize the limitations as well as the abilities of your dog, and the final product of your training zeal will bring you pride in accomplishment, pride in yourself and your ability, and pride in your Cocker.

156

XI

Training for the Show Ring

So many things of beauty or near perfection are so often marred and flawed by an improper approach to their finish. A Renoir or an El Greco tacked frameless to a bathroom wall is no less a thing of art, yet loses importance by its limited environment and presentation. Living things, too, need this finish and preparation to exhibit their worth to full advantage. The beauty of a flower goes unrecognized if withered petals and leaves mar its perfection, and the living wonder of a fine dog is realized only in those moments when he stands or moves in quiet and balanced beauty. The show ring is a ready frame in which to display your dog. The manner in which he is presented within that frame is up to you.

If you contemplate showing your Cocker, as so many of you who read this book do, it is of the utmost importance that your dog be as well and fully trained for exhibition as he is for general gentlemanly conduct in the home. Insufficient or improper training, or faulty handling, can result in lower show placings than your dog deserves and can quite conceivably ruin an otherwise promising show career. In the wider sense, and of even more importance to the breed as a whole, is the impression your Cocker in the show ring projects to the gallery. Every Cocker shown becomes a representative of the breed in the eyes of the onlookers, so that each dog becomes a symbol of all Cocker Spaniels when he is on exhibition. Inside the ring ropes, your dog will be evaluated by the judges as an individual; beyond

Pictured on the opposite page is the terrific black,
Ch. Treasure Hill Masterpiece, bred by M.
Cecelia Schmid, and owned by Maurice and Joan
Ferrero. Sired by Ch. Hickory Hill High
Bracket x Ch. Treasure Hill Dark Satin, this top
Cocker has been exclusively handled by
John Davidson.

the ropes, a breed will be judged by the behavior of your dog. So often the abominable behavior of an untrained animal irks even those whose interest lies with the breed. Think, then, what a warped impression of the breed must be conveyed, by this same animal, to the critically watching ringsider.

When you enter your Cocker in a show, you do so because you believe that he or she is a good enough specimen of the breed to afford competition to, and perhaps win over, the other dogs entered. If your dog is as good as you think he is, he certainly deserves to be shown to full advantage if you expect him to win or place in this highly competitive sport. A novice handler with a quality Cocker which is untrained, unruly, or phlegmatic cannot give competition to a dog of equal, or even lesser, merit which is well trained and handled to full advantage.

Novice owners frequently bring untrained dogs to shows so that they can become accustomed to the strange proceedings and surroundings, hopefully thinking that, in time, the dog will learn to behave in the wanted

It takes a lot of "know-how" to bring a Cocker Spaniel to the show ring groomed to win. Your dog must be trimmed and barbered to look his best, to hide faults and bring out virtues.

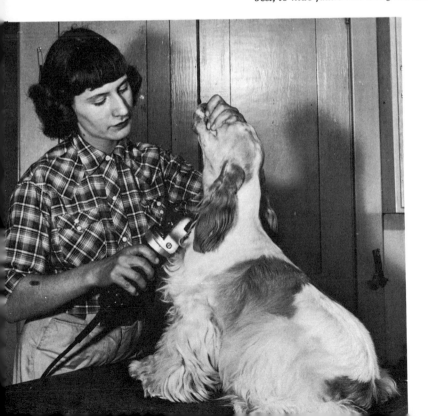

*The Cocker Spaniel's head is a thing of beauty,
and since it accounts for more than one quarter
of the total scale of points in judging it behooves
the owners to barber it with extreme care.*

manner by himself. Often the novice's training for the show ring begins in desperate and intense endeavor within the show ring itself. Confusion for both dog and handler can be the only result of such a program. Preparation for showing must begin long in advance of actual show competition for both dog and handler.

ADVANCE PREPARATION

Let us assume that you have been fortunate enough to breed or purchase a puppy who appears to possess all the necessary qualifications for a successful show career. Training for that career should begin from the moment you bring him home, or if you are the breeder, from the time he is weaned. This early training essentially follows the same pattern as does fundamental training in conduct. Again you begin by establishing between you and the puppy the happy relationship which, in time, becomes the control so necessary to all training. Handle the puppy frequently, brush him, examine his teeth, set him up in a show stance, and stroke his back slowly. Move him on a loose leash, talking to him constantly in a happy, friendly tone. Make all your movements in a deliberate and quiet manner. Praise and pat the puppy often, establishing an easy and happy rapport during this period. This is simple early preparation for the more exact training to come.

During this period the owner and prospective handler should take the opportunity to refresh or broaden his own knowledge. Reread the standard, and with this word picture in mind, build a mental reproduction of the perfect Cocker: his structure, balance, gait, and movement. Critically observe the better handlers at shows to see how they set and gait their dogs. Only by accumulating insight and knowledge such as this can you succeed in the training which will bring out the best features of your own future show dog.

SHOW GROOMING

It is time now to learn something of the art of show grooming or preparing, known to the professional as "putting down." For the novice it may be the better part of valor to allow a professional handler to do the initial job, observing the preparation closely and asking many "why" questions. The idea of the show preparation is to trim your dog to look his best, to follow the standard for the breed as closely as possible, and to hide faults and bring out virtues. The latter cannot be considered "faking". You are merely attempting to make your dog look as perfect as possible, and it is up to the judge to find the covered-up faults.

There are two schools of thought on what aids should be used for this beautification. One school (led generally by veterinarians) advocates the use of clippers (automatic) as an essential part of the implements to be used. The other school (recommended by professional handlers) abhors the use of clippers except when the coat has been allowed to get much out of hand. Then clippers can be used to get it down to manageable size where the razor stripper can be employed. Regardless of what means are used to do the job you must watch and learn so that you can, in time, do it yourself. It may be that you will find, when that time comes, that a combination of the implements of grooming sponsored by both basic schools will suit you well.

First supply yourself with a box or table, upon which to set your dog for grooming, that is of a nice height, suitable to allow you to go about your task without undue strain to back or legs through bending or squatting. Next arrange to attach a grooming arm that will jut over the table (or box) and to which you can clip a leash that, when attached to the dog's collar, will hold him in the best position to be groomed.

Above the groomer is trimming the Cocker's breeching with a scissors.
Below, the tail base is being scissored to pleasing shape.

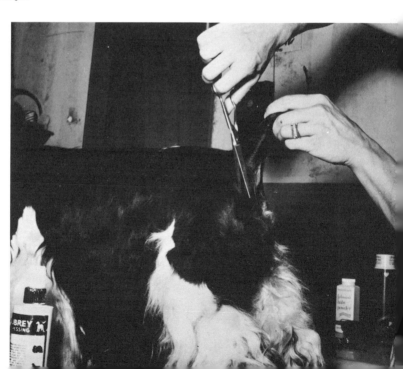

Now lay out your tools. You should have a steel comb with inch long teeth, about twelve teeth to the inch, a fairly stiff brush, a razor-blade dresser with plenty of new blades, barber's shears, an ordinary pair of curved shears (optional), nail clippers (guillotine type) and a file. Use the electric clipper if your dog is very wooly and always clip with, not against, the grain (from front to back).

Assuming that your Cocker's coat is not too heavy, or that you have clipped it down with the electric clippers to where it is manageable, start at the head with your razor and shave the skull clean and smooth. Carry your razor strokes down to the set-on of the ear, shortening the hair on the top of the ear down about one-and-a-half inches to accentuate the wanted low ear carriage. Clean the hair inside the ears close to the cheek so that the ear will hang close. Clean down the cheeks and under the neck where it attaches to the under jaw. Extend this cleaning down the whole neck and into the shoulders. Incidentally, when working on the head allow the eyebrows to remain thick, just trimming them even. This accentuates the stop. Clean the shoulders down to remove any coat thickness and "petticoats" that may give the shoulder an overloaded appearance. On the underside of the neck clean down to the base and allow the coat to arch in fullness from there. The neck, when cleaned, should appear long, graceful and with a slight arch.

Trim the backline so it is a smooth, sloping line from the withers to the set-on of the tail. Comb out the feathering on the legs and, with the scissors, trim it if too long or, if of correct length, merely even it up. Still using the scissors trim the feet to round fullness (large cat-foot) and remove any surplus foot hair between toes or under foot between pads. Feathering on the underbody should be evened and, if the dog is leggy more feather should be left than if he is short-legged or normal in leg length. Side feather on the legs should be removed so the bone looks straight. Feathering on the hind legs must be trimmed to neatness and to give the stifle flair and definite angulation at the hocks. With your scissor remove muzzle whiskers and all other long hair from this area and trim for squareness in the lips (be careful here, it is a delicate operation).

RING MANNERS

Now that our young show ring aspirant is trimmed and beautified, let us train him in show-ring deportment. The early training you have given him as a very young puppy to stand for handling is the basis from which you

Trimming the muzzle. All of the long muzzle hairs must be scissored off. Be careful not to point the sharp end of the shears toward the animal's eyes.

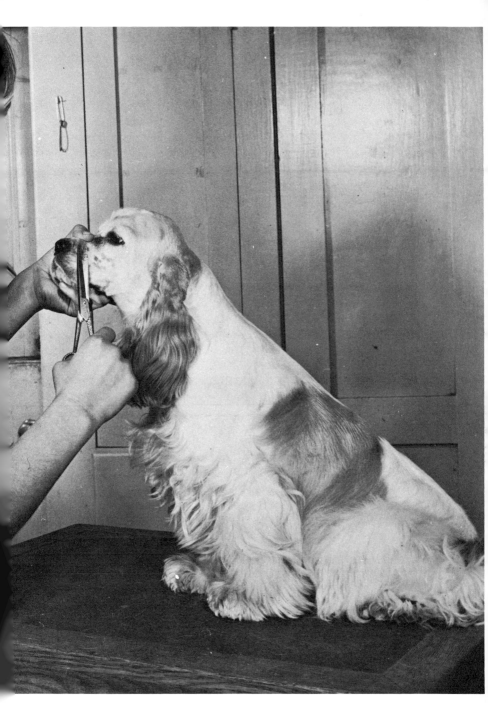

must work. Make him stand at your command. If his front legs aren't exactly right correct his stance by putting your hand under his chest directly behind the front legs, lifting and gently setting him down again into the right forehand position, with his legs straight and parallel. Next put your hand between his hindlegs and raise him and set him down so that his hindquarters slope back showing a good bend of stifle and with the hocks exactly vertical to the floor. Viewed from behind the legs should be straight. The position of the hind legs should also shape the back to a straight and sloping line to the tail.

Now raise your dog's head, square the muzzle by gently pulling the lips square, and pull the head forward so that the dog is looking slightly upward and, while posing, is throwing his weight on his forehand. Hold the leash high and smooth all neck flesh down so that the leash doesn't push it into a small lump under the chin. But be careful that you don't pull the ears up with the leash and make them appear higher set than they are. Make him also pose perfectly without the leash.

Teach him to hold this pose for ever longer periods of time with the reward of a tiny piece of some kind of tidbit. All the movements you make around the dog when setting him up, etc., must be done slowly and gently.

The feet should be trimmed with scissors. When correctly barbered they should appear thick, broad, and round.

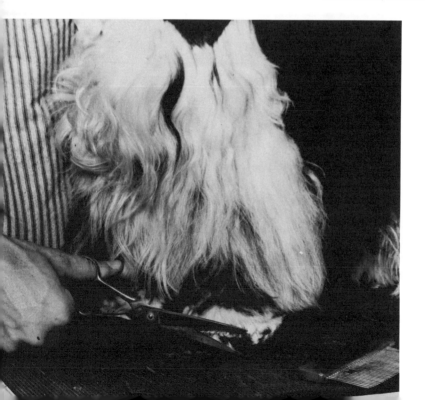

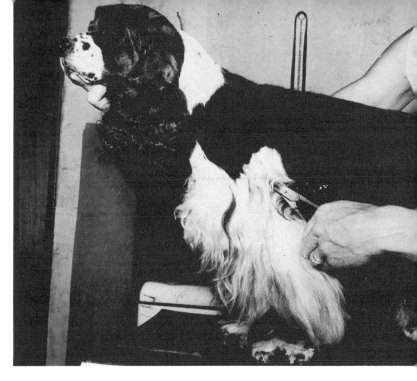

Thinning shears are being used here to get under the coat and thin beneath it to rectify a slightly loaded shoulder.

Never grab him by the tail to pick up his hindquarters; he will resent it and inevitably squat. Be patient and watch the better professional handlers and you will soon have your Cocker standing like a show ring veteran.

When you move your dog listen to the judge's directions when you are in the ring. When you are training your Cocker make him move straight and with small jerks of the lead make him keep his head up. The Cocker has a tendency to drop his nose to the ground when moving. Use the leash held straight and up away from your body so that it forms a fairly taut line, to foil his natural instincts and oblige him to keep his head raised as he moves trappily along. Once he has learned this lesson he should be taught to move on a loose leash with his head up, to swing along proudly and naturally. His gait and natural balance will be better than if he is "hung" up by a tight lead while moving, a practice much in vogue with handlers of sporting dogs.

When you come to the end of the allotted run and turn to start back, do not jerk the dog around; instead give him more leash freedom and allow him to come around easily without a change of leads, meanwhile speaking to him quietly. When he has completed the turn, draw him to you with the leash

A flat wire brush with short wire bristles should be used to comb the Cocker's ears. Do not dig so deeply that the skin (or leather) becomes irritated.

and continue moving back to the starting point. At the finish, pat and praise him.

While you are teaching your dog the elements of ring deportment, take stock of the pupil himself. To do this correctly, you will need assistance. Have someone else put the dog through his paces, handling him as you have and as he will be handled in the show ring. Observe the dog carefully to determine when he looks his best. Should he be stretched out a bit when posing? Or does he have better balance and outline if his hind legs are not pulled too far back? At what rate of speed, when moving, does he perform his best?

Pretend that you are a judge. Envision the perfect Cocker, and employing your knowledge of the standard as a yardstick, study your dog as though he were a strange animal. From this study you will see many things, tiny nuances, that will aid you in showing your Cocker to the best possible advantage in open competition.

166

*Ch. Juniper Jeweler. This splendid red dog is
shown going Best of Winners at Westminster.
He is handled by Ted Young, Jr. and owned by
Mrs. Violet Myshrall.*

Once he has mastered the show training you have given him, you must take every opportunity to allow strangers and friends to go over your dog, much in the manner of a judge, while you pose and gait him, so he will become used to a judge's unaccustomed liberties. It would be well to enter your Cocker in a few outdoor sanction matches now, to acquaint him with the actual conditions under which he will be shown. During all this time, of course, the character and temperament of your dog, as well as his physical assets, must be taken into consideration, as it must in all types of training, and the most made of the best he has.

It is of the utmost importance that you never become blind to your dog's faults, but at the same time realize his good features and attempt to exploit these when in the ring. Make sure your dog is in good physical shape, in good coat, clean and well groomed. If a bath is necessary, give it to him several days before the show so the natural oils will have time to smooth the coat and

STEPS IN STACKING A COCKER SPANIEL

FOR THE SHOW RING

Above: Front view of the dog being lifted to set front naturally. Right:

Another view (side) of the same basic maneuver. The dog is lifted by the muzzle and under the chest.

The dog has been dropped into position, head held up by the handler to hold the balance of the front assembly.

*Above: The Cocker's hock is being hand
positioned to be parallel to the ground and to
exhibit good angulation.
Below: The dog is now
set up (stacked) in an excellent show stance,
designed to exhibit the animal at its best.*

169

give it a natural sheen. Be sure he is not thirsty when he enters the ring and that he has emptied himself before showing, or it will cramp his movement and make him uncomfortable.

School yourself to be at ease in the ring when handling your dog, for if you are tense and nervous, it will communicate itself to the dog, and he will display the same emotional stress. In the ring, keep one eye on your dog and the other on the judge. One never knows when a judge might turn from the animal he is examining, look at your dog, and perhaps catch him in an awkward moment.

On the morning of the show, leave your home early enough so that you will have plenty of time to be benched and tend to any last minute details which may come up. When the class before yours is in the ring, give your dog a last quick brush, then run a towel over his coat to bring out the gloss. Should his coat be dull, a few drops of brilliantine, rubbed between the palms of your hands and then sparingly applied to the dog's coat, will aid in eliminating the dullness.

Bring to the show with you: a water pail, towel, brush, comb, suppositories in a small jar, a bench chain, and a light leash for showing. If the dog has not emptied himself, insert a suppository in his rectum when you take him to the exercising ring. If you forget to bring the suppositories, use instead two paper matches, wet with saliva, from which you have removed the sulphur tips.

Following is a chart listing the dog-show classes and indicating eligibility in each class with appropriate remarks. This chart will tell you at a glance which is the best class for your dog.

Showing the dog's teeth (bite) to the judge should be practiced long before the day the animal is to be exhibited. Be gentle and make a game of it.

CLASSES AND JUDGING

DOG-SHOW CLASS CHART

CLASS	ELIGIBLE DOGS	REMARKS
PUPPY—6 months and under 9 months	All puppies from 6 months up to 9 months.	Imports (except Canadian) not eligible for this class.
PUPPY—9 months and under 12 months	All puppies from 9 months to 12 months.	Imports (except Canadian) not eligible for this class.
NOVICE	Any dog or puppy which has not won an adult class (over 12 months), or any higher award, at a point show.	After three first-place Novice wins, cannot be shown again in the class. American- or Canadian-bred only.
BRED BY EXHIBITOR	Any dog or puppy, other than a Champion, which is owned and bred by exhibitor.	Must be shown only by a member of immediate family of breeder-exhibitor, *i.e.*, husband, wife, father, mother, son, daughter, brother, sister.
AMERICAN-BRED	All dogs or puppies whelped in the U.S. or possessions, except Champions, from a mating which took place in the U.S.	
OPEN DOGS	All dogs, 6 months of age or over, including Champions and foreign-breds.	Canadian and foreign champions are shown in open until acquisition of American title. By common courtesy, most American Champions are entered only in Specials.
SPECIALS CLASS	American Champions.	Compete for Best of Breed or Best of Variety, for which no points are given.

Each sex is judged separately. The winners of each class compete against each other for Winners and Reserve Winners. The animal designated as Winner is awarded the points. Reserve Winners receive no points. Reserve Winners can be the second dog in the class from which the Winners Dog was chosen. The Winners Male and Winners Female (Winners Dog and Winners Bitch) compete for Best of Winners. The one chosen Best of Winners competes against the Specials for Best of Variety, and the Best of Variety winner goes into the Sporting Group. If fortunate enough to top

171

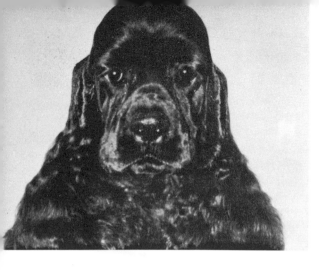

A lovely portrait of a fine young Cocker by the animal photographer, Liz.

this group, the final step is to compete against the other group winners for the Best in Show title.

When Best of Variety is awarded, Best of Opposite Sex is also chosen. A Cocker which has taken the points in its own sex as Winners, yet has been defeated for Best of Winners, can still be awarded Best of Opposite Sex if there are no animals of its sex appearing in the ring for the Best of Variety award.*

Champions are made by the point system. Only the Winners Dog and Winners Bitch receive points, and the amount of points won depends upon the number of Cockers of its own sex the dog has defeated in the classes (not by the number entered). The United States is divided into five regional point groups by the A.K.C., and the point rating varies with the region in which the show is held. Consult a show catalogue for regional rating. A Cocker going Best of Winners is allowed the same number of points as the

---

* In December of 1967 the dog show rules relative to the progression of the classes in judging were changed. After Reserve Winners has been chosen in bitches the Winners Dog and Winners Bitch both compete with any champions entered. The judge first chooses Best of Breed, then Best of Winners, and finally Best of Opposite Sex. In the event that one of the class dogs is chosen Best of Breed, it automatically becomes Best of Winners.

The Specials Class (for Champions only), no longer exists as such and has been renamed "For Best of Breed (Variety) Competition". This class is open to the Winners Dog, Winners Bitch, Champions of Record and dogs who have, according to their owners records, completed the requirements for a championship but have not as yet received confirmation of their status from the American Kennel Club. This latter category of dogs can compete for Best of Breed (or Variety) for a period of 90 days from the time they have ostensibly finished their championships.

Exhibiting how the show leash is slipped over the head of the dog.

animal of the opposite sex which it defeats if the points are of a greater amount than it won by defeating members of its own sex.

To become a Champion, a dog must win fifteen points under a minimum of three different judges. In accumulating these points, he must win points in at least two major (three points or more) shows, under different judges. Five points is the maximum amount that can be won at any given show. If your Cocker wins a group, he is entitled to the highest number of points won in any of the sporting breeds by the dogs he defeats in the group if the points exceed the amount he has won in his own breed. If the show is a Cocker Specialty, then the Best of Breed winner automatically becomes the Best in Show dog.

Cocker show classes have, besides the ordinary categories, divisions for the various colors. Solids compete against each other, partis have their own classes, and there are ASCOB (Any Solid Color Other Than Black) classes, the latter embracing the black-and-tan color phase. Blacks compete against other blacks. Study your official standard for a working knowledge of color classification.

The basic reason for the dog show, the object in the gathering together of representative animals of the breed in open competition, seems to have been mislaid in the headlong pursuit for ribbons, trophies, and points. These prizes undoubtedly lead to kennel-name popularity, which in turn produces greater and more profitable puppy sales and stud services, but they are not the end in themselves. They are given simply as tokens of achievement in a much larger pattern which has no direct relation to economy. The graded selection of various dogs according to individual quality by a competent, unbiased judge enables earnest breeders to weigh and evaluate the products of certain breedings and strains. It helps them to evaluate their own breeding procedures in relation to comparative quality, and to give them an idea as to which individuals, or breeding lines, can act as correctives to the faults inherent in their own breeding. Here the yardstick of the official standard is used to measure the defects or virtues of individual animals and of the breed as a whole for the edification and tabulation of both the knowing breeder and the novice. This is what a dog show should mean to the exhibitor.

Essentially the judge should be an intermediary between the present and the future, because his decisions shape the trends for better or for worse. If these trends lead to undesirable results, there will be deterioration instead of an ever-closer approach to the breed ideal. The judge is a sounding board, a calculator of degrees of excellence, an instrument for computing worth. He can, with each assignment, give something of enduring value toward breed improvement. As such, he or she must not only be entirely familiar with the standard, but must also understand every element of structure and balance. And almost more important, the judge must be able to see and evaluate each of those tiny nuances of quality which can establish the superiority of one animal over another of apparently equal excellence.

Though there are times when the judge is at fault, we must not forget that there are many times when the exhibitor's evaluation of the judge's placings is faulty. Too many exhibitors know too little about their own breed and are not competent to indulge in criticism. The very structure of dog-show procedure lends itself to dissatisfaction with the judge's decisions. The fact that there can be only a few really satisfied winners in any breed judging, Winner's Male, Winner's Bitch, and Best of Breed, and that they are chosen by one individual who may or may not be competent, leaves a wide range of just or unjust recrimination for the exhibitor to air. Some of the post-mortem denunciation can be attributed directly to the psychological effect of the shows upon the exhibitors themselves.

Many of the most prominent breeders who have been in the breed for years are judges as well. They are frequently criticized for their show-ring placements because they will put up animals of their own breeding or those of similar type to the strain they themselves produce. Undeniably, there are many instances in which a dog, handled or owned by an individual who is himself a judge, is given preference, since the breeder-judge officiating at the moment will, in the near future, show under the owner of the dog he has put up and expects the same consideration in return. This is but one of the many ways in which a judge may be influenced consciously or unconsciously. Regardless of the underlying cause, such practice must be condemned. But in most cases the breeder-judge who elevates animals of his own breeding or dogs of similar type cannot be summarily accused of lack of integrity. The type which he breeds must be the type he likes and his own interpretation of the standard. It follows, therefore, that this is the type he will put up in all honesty. We may question his taste, knowledge, or interpretation of the standard, but not, in most instances, his ethics or honesty.

There are, thank goodness, quite a few qualified and earnest judges whose placings should be followed and analyzed, for it is through them that we can evaluate the breeding health of the Cocker and know with confidence the individual worth of specific specimens. Judging is not an easy task. It does not generally lead to long and cozy friendships, for once an individual steps into the ring to begin his judiciary assignment, he is no longer an individual but becomes the impartial, wholly objective instrument of the standard. As such, friendship, personal likes or dislikes, cannot exist as facets of his make-up. He must judge the dogs before him as they are on that day without sentiment or favor. This is a task that demands complete subjection of self, high knowledge of the breed, and courage and integrity. It can be easily seen then, that not too many people could qualify in all these respects and so become completely proficient judges.

Were the ideal condition to exist, we, the breeders and owners, would submit our animals in open competition to the careful scrutiny of a truly competent authority whose integrity was beyond question. We would be able to compare our stock within the ring to see where we had erred. We would be able to measure the worth of breeding theory by the yardstick of a correct interpretation of the standard. We would know then what breeding lines were producing animals closest to the ideal and which individual dogs showed the highest degree of excellence; by thus creating, through the medium of the judge, an authority which we could depend upon, we could establish an easier path to the breed ideal.

Remember that showing dogs is a sport, not a matter of life and death. Tomorrow is another day, another show, another judge. The path of the show dog is never strewn with roses, though it may look that way to the novice handler who seems, inevitably, to step on thorns. Always be a good sport, don't run the other fellow's dog down because he has beaten yours, and when a Cocker goes into the group, give him your hearty applause even if you don't like the dog, his handler, his owner, and his breeding. Remember only that he is a Cocker Spaniel, a representative of your breed and therefore the best dog in the group.

We hope that this chapter will help the novice show handler to find greater ease and surety in training for show and handling in the ring and thus experience more pleasure from exhibiting. Competition is the spice of life, and a good Cocker should be shown to his best advantage, for his own glory and for the greater benefit of the breed.

XII

Training the Cocker Spaniel for the Field

The first and most important essential to gun dog training is a perfect understanding between dog and trainer. This *rapport* must be established early so that your Cocker puppy has complete and happy confidence in you, his master and trainer. Once this has been achieved you will always have your dog's eager attention and he will leap to obey your commands of voice, whistle and hand signal.

The general training you have given him will now come in handy. You have, through that fundamental training, established the control that is the basis of all training and now you and your Cocker can move easily into this new area of specialized education. The many commands you have taught

him to obey in the process of molding him into a proper house dog and companion will become stepping stones to his field training.

Perhaps the most important general trait we must make sure of in the gundog is his steadiness to sharp sounds, for a gun-shy Cocker is the epitome of uselessness in the field. Early training, the earlier the better, is the answer. If you have bred the litter yourself and the bitch, the dam of the puppies, is not gun-shy, you can begin making the puppies sound-sure during the weaning period. While the hungry little pups are gobbling up their food, fire a pistol of small calibre into the air at intervals and at a short distance from the pups. If they show no signs of disturbance from the reports, move closer to the puppies before firing. After a few times change to a rifle and later a shotgun, always starting at about the same distance away from them and lessening the distance with repetition until you can fire right over their heads without making them pause in their eating. The steadiness of their mother also acts as an example to the puppies.

The same procedure can be followed if you have a single, purchased, Cocker puppy. But, in this case first allow the youngster plenty of time to settle in, to be at home and confident in his new environment. Then, when the happy puppy is busily eating, fire the pistol. An alternate time to begin training for gun-sureness would be when the puppy is completely engrossed in happy play with someone in the family with whom he has fallen deeply in love . . . usually a youngster. The pup's playmate (or playmates) must be warned, of course, to evince no reaction to the sound of the gun.

Puppies love to chase and retrieve a thrown object. The big trouble here is that it is more play than serious work to retrieve and this attitude will be carried over into the time when the dummy is used and field training begins. To overcome this, make the pup sit at the "heel" position until given the command to fetch the dummy to hand. The "sit" or "hup" period is gradually lengthened until the Cocker realizes that the time of playing in this department is past and that the fetch is to be made only upon command.

Do not make your puppy work too long, and vary his work often so that he will not be driven to lackadaisical conduct through boredom engendered by repeating the same set of exercises for too long a period of time during one training session. Here again the earlier deportment training can be useful for, by utilizing familiar commands, many more and varied exercises can be indulged in to keep your puppy alert and eager.

Patience is a necessary virtue that must be developed by the trainer. Some puppies take much more time to develop than others. Today, due to the many field trials throughout the country, there is a tendency to push, to try to develop the young dog quickly for the Derbies. This can ruin a good young dog that is a slow developer. Many trainers forget that field trial dogs are asked to do much more than they did a few years ago, and the competition is much tougher. Often professional handlers are obsessed with the idea that there is no limit to what a young dog can and should do regardless of the shortness of the training period. The result of such training philosophy is the turning out of a few very good dogs (on which to pin their reputation) along with a vastly greater number of mediocre animals which could have been excellent field dogs if they had been given more time to develop and learn.

The puppy who is slow to develop, who shows no desire or interest in his work, cannot be forced. It is best to work this type of puppy with an older dog. Frequently the youngster's interest will be aroused by the antics of the older dog and he will begin to imitate. Keep this type of puppy with you as much as possible when you are working other dogs so that he can watch and, you hope, eventually become aware of his responsibility to you and to his heritage.

Sometimes a puppy who is doing beautifully will suddenly seem to lose interest in the whole proceeding. Don't try to force him. Instead, give him a short vacation from all training. Generally, when you bring him out again, he will work with zest and vigor and grasp new lessons with greater rapidity than before.

Dogs, like children, must be chastised immediately when they do wrong. You will generally find that your Cocker puppy is sensitive enough to be chastised through verbal scoldings and the vocal sharpness of your voiced

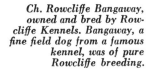

Ch. Rowcliffe Bangaway, owned and bred by Rowcliffe Kennels. Bangaway, a fine field dog from a famous kennel, was of pure Rowcliffe breeding.

displeasure. Occasionally you may have to deal with the stubborn, insensitive dog who can take physical chastisement without undue mental disturbance. But remember that many dogs have been spoiled by the wrong kind and intensity of discipline. Only scold or forcibly correct the puppy when he can be caught in the act of disobeying. If, for example, your Cocker breaks before command and retrieves the object (or bird) and delivers it to you in retrieve, he should not be punished for he will think that he is being punished for retrieving and returning the object to hand. Catch him as he breaks before the command releasing him and before he reaches the object to be retrieved. Scold him and make him obey and not leave before he has been released by your command for the retrieve.

Most of all, remember never to lose your own temper. All chastisement must be done methodically and coldly and not while in the throes of anger. If you can't control yourself you will never be able to control your dog.

Puppies, during the early training period, will sometimes exhibit various exasperating traits and habits. Most of these will disappear with experience and, by indulging in restraint and patience, the trainer will usually find that the puppy will correct himself and lose his early mischievousness with time and increasing interest in his work.

Double dummy retrieves often take the dog a bit of time to learn but, like anything else he must learn, don't go on to other lessons when he can

Three parti-colored American Cockers, an English Cocker and three Springers, all very capably handled by members of the Ladies Amateur Spaniel Handler's Association. The ladies are, from left to right, Ruth Greening, Mrs. Albert Winslow, and Gene Hutchins.

do this retrieve "pretty well." Be sure that this and every other lesson is learned thoroughly and executed with efficiency before going on to the next one.

Use the whistle as a call and it will teach your Cocker to quickly respond to whistle signals. For the recall use a long blast followed quickly by two short ones. Use this recall signal during very early training, to call the small puppy to his meals, to play and to call him in when walking and you wish to change direction. A single whistle blast is the "stop" and the "sit" or "hup" signal. In the field the recall is used to bring the dog all the way in, or to bring him in closer until he reaches the point where you wish to stop him and send him in another direction.

The whistle is also the means by which you get your dog's attention so that you can direct him with hand signals. Whistle and hand signals are the means by which you control the trained dog in the field. But, a word of warning! Do not overdo whistle and hand signals or you will develop a dog that is a mechanical hunter depending on you for his every move. Instead allow your dog leeway to use his nose and his inherited ability in the field so that he will seek and find game by himself and mark his birds and retrieve with a minimum of effort on your part, thus making his work in the field a greater pleasure to both himself and you, his master. Incidentally, during training, never send your dog to a spot (with whistle and hand signals) where there is nothing to find. He will become unsure and lose his sharpness when working.

In training to retrieve we must have the absolute control over our Cocker mentioned earlier in this chapter because of the fact that the Cocker is a Spaniel, and therefore a flushing dog, who will most likely flush the game away from the handler. He must, therefore, be steadied at a distance, for he must stop to flush, be steady to wing and shot, and then start the retrieve from the steadied or "hup" position instead of at the handler's side. The excitement of the scent and flush makes it imperative that control must be absolute if it is to be maintained from a distance.

Don't forget to constantly, and with conviction and enthusiasm, praise your dog for a correct performance. From you, the one he loves, this is more important to your Cocker than any other pleasure on earth.

Sometimes we come to a sticking point with a dog where it seems that we cannot improve him in some part of his field education in which he does badly. When this happens try to assess the dog from another angle. Ask yourself what you may have done to cause the dog to object to this part of his education. Perhaps you have tried to force him in water work when the water was too cold. He should have been started during warm weather, taken in to swim with you, so that he liked the water and forgot physical discomfort when he was ready for water training in the cold autumn. Physical discomfort is often the reason for a dog's reluctant behavior. A short-legged Cocker, or one too small, or weak in the jaws, will occasionally not take kindly to retrieving simply because it is a difficult job for him due to his physical shortcomings.

Sometimes, forcing a dog when he is too young or not yet ready will develop objectionable habits that will be difficult to overcome later. At five months you can teach your puppy the "Hup," "Sit," "Fetch," "Seek," and take him into warm summer water. But wait until his inherent love for hunting makes itself obvious before attempting to make him obey these commands in actual field work.

Of course the will to work, the necessary drive, fleetness, determination and courage must be part of the dog's inheritance. Sometimes proper training will bring these traits to the fore but, if they are not there to begin with they cannot be developed to any great extent, that is, to the extent where a dog who lacks these traits to a degree but has been cannily trained, can be a competitive factor in a field trial.

Remember this, a good field trial dog is a good hunting dog. Puppy trials are a wonderful way to select the worthwhile animals to work with for the later mature trials. Competition such as this is fun as well as profitable. You will be able to see where your puppy errs and needs more work and correction. It will give you a chance to review what you have done and why.

The various, important essentials that a judge looks for at field trials are the key to what we want in a gun dog. They are: 1. *Natural ability*; to mark the fall of game, to exhibit a natural interest in and understanding of field work so that he (the Cocker) will hunt with method and intelligence. 2. *Nose*; the game must be found by the dog, not the handler and to do this the dog must show scent discrimination. If he does not possess a good nose the judge will eventually eliminate him. 3. *Mouth*; he must have a tender mouth and not injure the game in any way when retrieving. 4. *Retrieving*; should be done efficiently, quickly and to hand. A dog who persistently drops the game or mouths it, will be penalized severely. 5. *Control*; the Cocker should be under absolute control so he can give instant obedience to all commands and directions from his handler, and not only at heel or to shot. A dog breaking shot or running in is eliminated from competition. 6. *Deportment*; the dog should perform with style and speed denoting interest and happiness in his work. He must work with the least disturbance of ground and as quietly as possible.

What do we have as an end result of proper selection and training for hunting or field trial competition? We have a sturdy, strong, up-to-size Cocker with a hunting heritage who is eager, in fact really lives, for the chance to work. He works with his tail up and in motion, keeping one eye on his handler as he works to the gun, and drives through any kind of terrain without hesitation. He will shift his work pattern to take advantage of the wind to catch any game scent it may carry. He will drive into the game cover, flush it to the gun, drop and remain there until the game is shot then, upon command, he will retrieve the game, whose fall he has marked, and bring it back, undamaged, to hand. If the cover is too heavy to mark the fall of game exactly the dog will move out in the direction of the fall and take assistance from his handler by hand and whistle directional signals to find the dead or wounded game. If the game is only wounded and runs, the dog

A good gun dog, a fine crisp day, and a nice pair of pheasants as the end result, a combination calculated to stir the heart of any sportsman or dog lover. The lucky man is Hartwell S. Moore, one of the foremost supporters of the American Cocker in the field. The dog is Field Ch. Berol's Buckaroo.

Above is a nice type red dog that is also a very handy dog in the field, and a marvelous family pet. Correct breeding and training are the twin necessities to give your Cocker type, temperament, intelligence and ability. Below a Cocker is retrieving to hand, an attribute all good flushing Spaniels must enjoy.

will pick up the scent and trail the moving game until he reaches it, retrieves it, and brings it in.

Initial training essentials are outlined here but, for advanced training, trailing, correcting hard mouths and retrieving mistakes, retrieving live and dead game, water work, all the many tricks and intricacies employed by professional trainers for specific correction and finish, there are other good books, dedicated specifically to field training and containing valuable information that cannot be incorporated in a book such as this one which deals with all the myriad facets of a specific breed.

All you who have Cockers remember this, your Cocker was originally developed as a sporting breed. Only a few of the many dogs bred each year have that absolute beauty and physical perfection and finish to become successful show dogs. Many, many more make, and are used for, fine family companions and pets. But to deny the Cocker the privilege of his basic heritage as a gun dog in the field, is to steal from him a major part of his reason for being. And it denies you, his owner, the rare and heart-warming pleasure of working with your dog in the out-of-doors, of sharing this wonderful closeness with him as he works, in all his specific glory, in the field, doing what comes naturally to the finest little sporting dog in the world, the Cocker Spaniel.

*This lovely bitch is American and Canadian
Champion, Flo-Bob's Born-A-Star, being handled
to Best-In-Show at the Walla Walla K.C. Show by
James Hall under judge Frances O. Holland.
The breeders and owners of Star are the
Flo-Bob Kennels.
sire: Ch. Holly Tree Born-A-Star
dam: Am. & Can. Ch. Flo-Bob's High Time*

XIII

Official Standard of the Cocker Spaniel

SKULL: Well developed and rounded with no tendency toward flatness, or pronounced roundness, of the crown (dome). The forehead smooth, the eyebrows and stop clearly defined, the median line distinctly marked and gradually disappearing until lost rather more than halfway up to the crown. The bony structure surrounding the socket of the eye should be well chiseled; there should be no suggestion of fullness under the eyes or prominence in the cheeks which, like the sides of the muzzle, should present a smooth, clean-cut appearance.

MUZZLE AND TEETH: To attain a well-proportioned head, which above all should be in balance with the rest of the dog, the distance from the tip of the nose to the stop, at a line drawn across the top of the muzzle between the front corners of the eyes, should approximate one-half the distance from the stop at this point up over the crown to the base of the skull. The muzzle should be broad and deep, with square, even jaws. The upper lip should be of sufficient depth to cover the lower jaw, presenting a square appearance. The teeth should be sound and regular and set at right angles to their respective jaws. The relation of the upper teeth to the lower should be that of scissors, with the inner surface of the upper in contact with the outer surface of the lower when the jaws are closed. The nose of sufficient size to balance the muzzle and foreface, with well-developed nostrils, and black in color in the blacks and black and tans; in the reds, buffs, livers, and parti-colors, and in the roans it may be black or brown, the darker coloring being preferable.

EYES: The eyeballs should be round and full and set in the surrounding tissue to look directly forward and give the eye a slightly almond-shaped appearance. The eye should be neither weak nor goggled. The expression should be intelligent, alert, soft and appealing. The color of the iris should be dark brown to black in the blacks, black and tans, buffs and creams, and in the darker shades of the parti-colors and roans. In the reds, dark hazel; in the livers, parti-colors, and roans of the lighter shades, not lighter than hazel, the darker the better.

EARS: Lobular, set on a line no higher than the lower part of the eye, the leather fine and extending to the nostrils, well clothed with long, silky, straight or wavy hair.

NECK AND SHOULDERS: The neck sufficiently long to allow the nose to reach the ground easily, muscular and free from pendulous "throatiness." It should rise strongly from the shoulders and arch slightly as it tapers to join the head. The shoulders deep, clean-cut and sloping without protrusion and so set that the upper points of the withers are at an angle which permits a wide spring of rib.

BODY: Its height at the withers should approximate the length from the withers to the set-on of tail. The chest deep, its lowest point no higher than the elbows, its front sufficiently wide for adequate heart and lung space, yet not so wide as to interfere with straightforward movement of the forelegs. Ribs deep and well-sprung throughout. Body short in the couplings and flank, with its depth at the flank somewhat less than at the last rib. Back strong and sloping evenly and slightly downward from the withers to the set-on of tail. Hips wide with quarters well-rounded and muscular. The body should appear short, compact and firmly knit together, giving the impression of strength.

This photo is used to give the reader an idea of the wooly type of coat sported by some Cocker Spaniels. Such a coat must be drastically barbered to meet the qualifications of the standard.

EXTERNAL ANATOMY OF THE COCKER SPANIEL

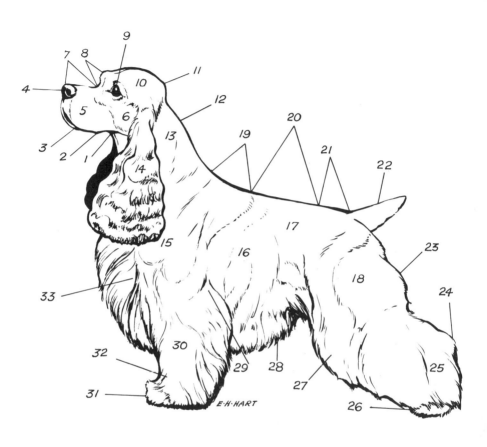

1. *Throat.* 2. *Lip corner (flew).* 3. *Under jaw.*
4. *Nose.* 5. *Muzzle.* 6. *Cheek.* 7. *Foreface.* 8. *Stop.*
9. *Eye.* 10. *Skull.* 11. *Occiput.* 12. *Crest (of neck).*
13. *Neck.* 14. *Ear (leather).* 15. *Shoulder.* 16. *Ribs
(ribbing).* 17. *Loin.* 18. *Thigh.* 19. *Withers.* 20.
Back. 21. *Croup.* 22. *Tail (stern).* 23. *Feathering.*
24. *Hock joint.* 25. *Hock.* 26. *Feet.* 27. *Stifle.* 28.
Bottom line. 29. *Elbow.* 30. *Forearm.* 31. *Feet
(paws).* 32. *Pastern.* 33. *Forechest.*

LEGS AND FEET: Forelegs, straight, strongly boned and muscular, and set close to the body well under the scapulae. The elbows well let down and turning neither in nor out. The pasterns short and strong. The hind legs strongly boned and muscled with well-turned stifles and powerful, clearly defined thighs. The hocks strong, well let down and paralleled when in motion and at rest. Feet compact, not spreading, round and firm, with deep, strong, horny pads and hair between the toes; they should turn neither in nor out.

TAIL: Set on and carried on a line with the topline of the back and when the dog is at work, its action should be incessant.

1. Excellent Cocker front. 2. Too narrow, feet east and west. 3. Barrel legged, loaded in shoulder.

COAT: On head, short and fine. On body, flat or slightly wavy (never curly), silky in texture, of medium length, with enough undercoating to give protection. The ears, chest, abdomen, and posterior sides of the legs should be well feathered, but not so excessively as to hide the Cocker Spaniel's true lines and movement or affect his appearance and function as a sporting dog. Excessive coat or feathering shall be penalized.

COLOR AND MARKINGS: Blacks should be jet black; shadings of brown or liver in the sheen of the coat shall not disqualify; but shall be penalized. A small amount of white on the chest and throat shall not disqualify, but shall be penalized; however, white on any other location shall disqualify.

Solid Colors Other Than Black should be of a sound shade. Lighter coloring of the feathering, while not favored, shall not disqualify. A small amount of white on the chest and throat shall not disqualify, but shall be penalized; however, white in any other location shall disqualify.

In Parti-Colors, at least two definite colors appearing in clearly defined markings, distinctively distributed over the body, are essential. Primary color which is ninety (90%) per cent or more of the specimen, shall disqualify; secondary color or colors which are limited solely to one location shall disqualify. Roans are classified as Parti-Colors and may be of the accepted roaning patterns of mottled appearance or alternating colors of the hairs throughout the whole coat.

Black and Tan, shown under the Variety of Any Solid Color Other Than Black, should have definite tan markings on a jet black body, with clearly defined lines between the two colors. The tan markings should be distinct and plainly visible, and the shade of the tan markings may be from the lightest

1. *Excellent rear quarters of Cocker.* 2. *Badly cowhocked.*

cream to the darkest red color. The quantity and location of the tan markings are the essence of this description. The amount of tan markings is restricted to ten (10%) per cent or less of the color of the specimen; tan markings in excess of ten (10%) per cent shall disqualify. A mere semblance of tan markings at the specified locations shall not disqualify, but shall be severely penalized; the total absence of tan markings at any of the specified locations, shall disqualify. The markings should be located as follows:

(1) A clear spot over each eye. (2) On the sides of the muzzle, and on the cheeks. (3) On the undersides of the ears. (4) On all feet and legs. (5) Under the tail.

Tan on the muzzle which extends up and over and joins, or tan on the cheeks which is solid, or tan on the feet which does not extend upward towards the knees and hock joints, shall not disqualify, but shall be penalized. Black hairs and penciling on the tan markings shall not be penalized, but tan markings which are "brindled" shall be penalized. A small amount of

1. *Roach back; shoulder too far forward; too much bend in pastern; lack of hindquarter angulation; tail too short; mutton withers (flat); lacks flare in stifle; too leggy.*

2. *Wet throat; head planes not parallel, comparatively short neck; sway back; croup too rounded and drops off; tail set too low; too long in loin; too short in leg; common in head.*

BONE STRUCTURE OF A COCKER SPANIEL

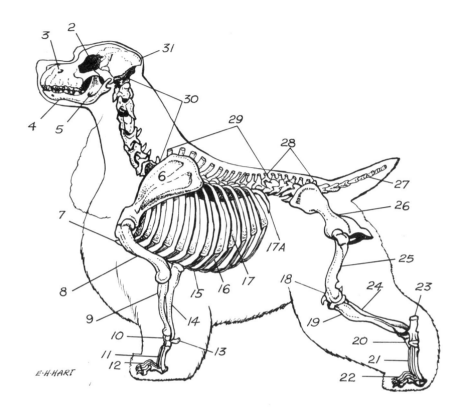

E·H·HART

1. *Cranium (skull)*. 2. *Orbital cavity*. 3. *Nasal bone*. 4. *Mandible (jaw bone)*. 5. *Condyle*. 6. *Scapula (shoulder blade)*. 7. *Prosternum*. 8. *Humerus (upper arm)*. 9. *Radius (front forearm bone)*. 10. *Carpus (pastern joint, comprised of 7 bones)*. 11. *Metacarpus (pastern, comprised of 5 bones)*. 12. *Phalanges (digits or toes)*. 13. *Pisiform (accessory carpal bone)*. 14. *Ulna*. 15. *Sternum (cartilage)*. 16. *Costal Cartilage*. 17. *Rib bones*. 18. *Patella (knee joint)*. 19. *Tibia (with fibula comprises shank bone)*. 20. *Tarsus (seven bones)*. 21. *Metatarsus (five bones)*. 22. *Phalanges (toes, digits)*. 23. *Oscalcis (point of hock)*. 24. *Fibula*. 25. *Femur (thigh bone)*. 26. *Pelvic girdle*. 27. *Coccygeal vertebra (tail bones)*. 28. *Lumbar vertebra*. 29. *Thoracic vertebra*. 30. *Cervical vertebra*. 31. *Occiput*.

white on the chest and throat shall not disqualify, but shall be penalized. However, white in any other location shall disqualify.

HEIGHT: The ideal height at the withers for an adult dog should be 15 inches. The ideal height at the withers for an adult bitch should be 14 inches. The maximum height at the withers for a dog shall be 15½ inches and the maximum height at the withers for a bitch shall be 14½ inches. A dog or bitch whose height exceeds the maximum heights specified herein shall be disqualified. Note: Height is determined by a line perpendicular to the ground from the tip of the shoulder blades, the dog standing naturally with its

An informal shot of Ch. Winsome Way's Toby and friend. The quality of this excellent parti is evident in this unposed photo.

forelegs and the lower hind legs parallel to the line of measurement.

GENERAL DESCRIPTION: Embodying the foregoing we have a serviceable-looking dog with a refinedly chiseled head; standing on straight legs and well up at the shoulders; of compact body and wide, muscular quarters. The Cocker Spaniel's sturdy body, powerful quarters and strong, well-boned legs show him to be a dog capable of considerable speed combined with great endurance. Above all he must be free and merry, sound, well balanced throughout, and in action show a keen inclination to work; equable in temperament with no suggestion of timidity.

*Above is a studio portrait of Ch. Sirdar
Gobetween, owned by Mrs. George A. Carruthers.
This very masculine stud was by Ch. My Own
Again x Ch. Craigden Comely.*

*Below, owned by Mardomere Kennels and bred
by H. E. Mellenthin, is Ch. My Own Right Of
Way. Whelped in 1931, this dog was sired by the
famous, Red Brucie out of My Own Now-Or-Never.
Another of the top ones from the My Own
Kennels sired by Brucie.*

SCALE OF POINTS

Skull	8	Legs	9
Muzzle	10	Feet	6
Teeth	4	Stern	3
Eyes	6	Coat	6
Ears	3	Color and Markings	3
Neck and Shoulders	15	Action	12
Body	15		
		Total	100

Ch. Bobb's Master Showman, a grand parti-color of an earlier era in Cocker history. This dog was rich in Idahurst breeding.

DISQUALIFICATIONS

Color and Markings: Blacks—White markings except on chest and throat. Solid Colors Other Than Black—White markings except on chest and throat. Parti-Colors—Ninety (90%) per cent or more of primary color; secondary color or colors limited solely to one location. Black and Tans—Tan markings in excess of ten (10%) per cent; total absence of tan markings at any of the specified locations; white markings except on chest and throat. Height: males over $15\frac{1}{2}$ inches; females over $14\frac{1}{2}$ inches.

Approved December 10, 1957

A *standard* is a written analysis of a breed. The essence of its combined perfections present to the reader a word picture of a mythical superdog

Above is Ch. Brookside Brilliance, whelped in
1927 and owned by Mr. and Mrs. George Greer.
This is another fine Cocker sired by the
redoubtable Red Brucie. The dam of Brilliance
was Ch. Brookside Brunette.

The grand parti below, Ch. Sinaloa Moonshine,
1928, had a tremendous show career on the coast,
taking three Best In Show awards and nineteen
times Best Sporting.
sire: Jack of Dara   *dam: Bellmore Brazen.*

toward which the fanciers must strive. In its entirety, the standard disciplines in selection and rejection toward an ethical center or objective, which is the betterment of the breed.

There have been many who have complained that the standard, as it exists today, is too wordy and unwieldy. Others have suggested that a condensed version be printed for the use of judges, to be used by them in the nature of a freshener prior to judging assignments. Perhaps a better choice of words, in some few instances, would aid in shortening the standard as written, but not to any appreciable extent. It was evidently the purpose of those who were instrumental in fashioning the standard to make it so clear and concise that the reader could, as closely as the written word permits, visualize the ideal. In this design they were eminently successful to the degree that such a document can be successful. Any failure of the reader to know our breed in all its detail does not reflect upon the standard. Rather, it can be blamed upon lack of visual imagination, or faulty interpretation of

American and Canadian Ch. Abbis Mister A.O.K. taking his third Best In Show, owned and ably handled by Mrs. Harry Reno.

Ch. Champel's Sumpin' Flashy (black and tan,
ASCOB) owner-breeder Elizabeth H. Ahrens,
being handled by Thomas E. Campbell to a top
win under judge M. Baker.
sire: Ch. Valli-Lo's Flash A'Way
dam: Champel's Certainly Sumpin'

the written word by the reader. Standards can be too short or too vague, omitting succinct details that, in essence, differentiate the particular breed from all other breeds. A standard is never too long if it is concise and functionally complete. As it exists, it is a worth-while word picture of the breed.

A standard should not be considered rigid and unchangeable. Time brings faults and virtues to a breed which must be recognized and the standard changed in certain particulars to accommodate new values. Since the standard is a yardstick for the show ring and the breeder, evaluation of new trends should be qualified not only by cosmetic application, but by genetic implication as well. Thus, faults which are of an inheritable nature should be penalized far more severely than those which are transient.

A healthy dog is a happy dog and a pleasure to
the family to whom he belongs. Your veterinarian
is your dog's best friend, and can be yours, too,
particularly if there are children in your home,
for then the health of your Cocker is doubly
important.

XIV

Diseases and First Aid

The dog is heir to many illnesses, and, as with man, it seems that when one dread form has been overcome by some specific medical cure, another quite as lethal takes its place. It is held by some that this cycle will always continue, since it is nature's basic way of controlling specie population.

There are, of course, several ways to circumvent Dame Nature's lethal plans. The initial step in this direction is to put the health of your dogs in the hands of one who has the knowledge and equipment, mental and physical, to competently cope with your canine health problems. We mean, of course, a modern veterinarian. Behind this man are years of study and experience and a knowledge of all the vast research, past and present, which has developed the remarkable cures and artificial immunities that have so drastically lowered the canine mortality rate as of today.

Put your trust in the qualified veterinarian and "beware of Greeks bearing gifts." Beware, too, of helpful friends who say, "I know what the trouble is and how to cure it. The same thing happened to my dog." Home doctoring by unskilled individuals acting upon the advice of unqualified "experts" has killed more dogs than distemper.

Your Cocker is constantly exposed to innumerable diseases through the medium of flying and jumping insects, parasites, bacteria, fungus, and virus. His body develops defenses and immunities against many of these diseases, but there are many more which we must cure or immunize him against if they are not to prove fatal.

I am not qualified to give advice about treatment for the many menaces to your dog's health that exist and, by the same token, you are not qualified to treat your dog for these illnesses with the skill or knowledge necessary for success. I can only give you a resumé of modern findings on the most prevalent diseases and illnesses so that you can, in some instances, eliminate them or the causative agent yourself. Even more important, this chapter will help you recognize their symptoms in time to seek the aid of your veterinarian.

Though your dog can contract disease at any time or any place, he or she is most greatly exposed to danger when in the company of other dogs at dog shows or in a boarding kennel. Watch your dog carefully after it has been hospitalized or sent afield to be bred. Many illnesses have an incubation period, during the early stages of which the animal himself may not show the symptoms of the disease, but can readily contaminate other dogs with which he comes in contact. It is readily seen, then, that places where many dogs are gathered together, such as those mentioned above, are particularly dangerous to your dog's health.

Parasitic diseases, which we will first investigate, must not be taken too lightly, though they are the easiest of the diseases to cure. Great suffering and even death can come to your dog through these parasites that prey on him if you neglect to realize the importance of both cure and the control of reinfestation.

Ch. Winsome Way's Toby, shown going Best Of Breed. Toby is owned by Mrs. James H. Shackleton, Jr., Winsome Way Kennels. This handsome parti's sire is Ch. Scioto Bluff's Sinbad, his dam, Ch. Winsome Way's Cricket.

The fine black dog, Ch. Pinefair Password, going
Best In Show at the Wallkill Kennel Club, 1966.
He is owned by Mrs. H. Terrell Van Ingen, and
handled by Ted Young, Jr. The judge under whom
he made this win was Mrs. Marjorie Siebern.

EXTERNAL PARASITES

The lowly flea is one of the most dangerous insects from which you must protect your dog. It carries and spreads tapeworm, heartworm and bubonic plague, causes loss of coat and weight, spreads skin disease, and brings untold misery to its poor host. These pests are particularly difficult to combat because their eggs—of which they lay thousands—can lie dormant for months, hatching when conditions of moisture and warmth are present. Thus you may think you have rid your dog (and your house) of these devils, only to find that they mysteriously reappear as weather conditions change.

When your dog has fleas, use any good commercial flea powder which contains fresh rotenone. Dust him freely with the powder. It is not necessary to cover the dog completely, since the flea is active and will quickly reach a spot saturated with the powder and die. Rotenone is also fatal to lice. A solution of this drug in pine oil and added to water to be employed as a dip or rinse will kill all insects except ticks. DDT in liquid soap is excellent and

long-potent, its effect lasting for as long as a week. Benzene hexochloride, chlordane, and any number of many new insecticides developed for the control of flies are also lethal to fleas. Whatever specific is prescribed by your veterinarian should also be used on your dog's sleeping quarters as well as on the animal itself. Repeat the treatment in ten days to eliminate fleas which have been newly hatched from dormant eggs.

Chlorinated hydrocarbons (DDT, chlordane, dieldrin, etc.) are long acting. Organic phosphoriferous substances, such as Malathion, are quick killers with no lasting effect.

TICKS

There are many kinds of ticks, all of which go through similar stages in their life process. At some stage in their lives they all find it necessary to feed on blood. Luckily, these insect vampires are fairly easily controlled. The female of the species is much larger than the male, which will generally be found hiding under the female. Care must be taken in the removal of these pests to guard against the mouth parts remaining embedded in the host's skin when the body of the tick is removed. DDT is an effective tick remover. Ether or nail-polish remover, touched to the individual tick, will cause it to relax its grip and fall off the host. The heated head of a match from which the flame has been just extinguished, employed in the same fashion, will cause individual ticks to release their hold and fall from the dog. After

Ch. Chadori's Kiss Of Fire, a beautiful red bitch owned by Charles F. Olson. She is pictured going Best Puppy, American Spaniel Club, Zone III, 1963, handled by Ted Young, Jr., under judge, Mrs. H. Terrell Van Ingen.

veterinary tick treatment, no attempt should be made to remove the pests manually, since the treatment will cause them to drop by themselves as they succumb. Chlorinated hydrocarbons are very effective tick removers.

MITES

There are three basic species of mites that generally infect dogs, the demodectic mange mite (red mange), the sarcoptic mange mite (white mange), and the ear mite. Demodectic mange is generally recognized by balding areas on the face, cheeks, and the front parts of the forelegs, which present a moth-eaten appearance. Reddening of the skin and great irritation occurs as a result of the frantic rubbing and scratching of affected parts by the animal. Rawness and thickening of the skin follows. Not too long ago this was a dread disease in dogs, from which few recovered. It is still a persistent and not easily cured condition unless promptly diagnosed and diligently attended to.

Sarcoptic mange mites can infest you as well as your dog. The resulting disease is known as scabies. This disease very much resembles dry dermatitis, or what is commonly called "dry eczema." The coat falls out and the denuded area becomes inflamed and itches constantly.

Ear mites*, of course, infest the dog's ear and can be detected by an ac-

* Otodectic mange.

Ted Young, Jr., handling the top buff dog, Ch. Pinefair Pirate, to a Best Of Variety at the Eastern Dog Club Show of 1958. The dog is owned by Mrs. H. Terrell Van Ingen, and was put up by judge Herbert Roling.

cumulation of crumbly dark brown or black wax within the ear. Shaking of the head and frequent scratching at the site of the infestation accompanied by squeals and grunting also is symptomatic of the presence of these pests. Canker of the ear is a condition, rather than a specific disease, which covers a wide range of ear infection and which displays symptoms similar to ear mite infection.

All three of these diseases and ear canker should be treated by your veterinarian. By taking skin scrapings or wax particles from the ear for microscopic examination, he can make an exact diagnosis and recommend specific treatment. The irritations caused by these ailments, unless immediately controlled, can result in loss of appetite and weight, and so lower your dog's natural resistance that he is open to the attack of other diseases which his bodily defenses could normally battle successfully.

INTERNAL PARASITES

It seems strange, in the light of new discovery of specific controls for parasitism, that the incidence of parasitic infestation should still be almost as great as it was years ago. This can only be due to lack of realization by the dog owner of the importance of initial prevention and control against reinfestation. Strict hygiene must be adhered to if dogs properly treated are not to be exposed to infestation immediately again. This is particularly true where worms are concerned.

In attempting to rid our dogs of worms, we must not be swayed by amateur opinion. The so-called "symptoms" of worms may be due to many other reasons. We may see the actual culprits in the animal's stool, but even then it is not wise to worm indiscriminately. The safest method to pursue is to take a small sample of your dog's stool to your veterinarian. By a fecal analysis he can advise just what specific types of worms infest your dog and what drugs should be used to eliminate them.

Most puppies have some kind of internal parasites that must be eradicated. Your veterinarian will know how and when to accomplish this. The puppies shown here are "Flip" and "Dolly" at eight weeks of age, from Elizabeth H. Ahrens' Champel Kennels.

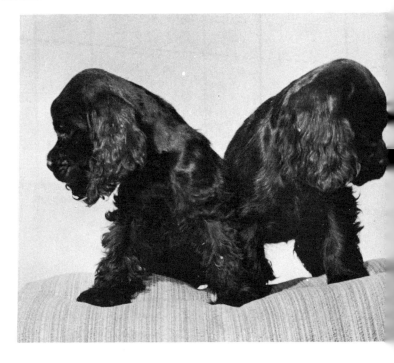

A top winning dog, the excellent black Cocker, Ch. Pinefair Password, is shown here by Ted Young, Jr., capturing sporting group honors at the Trenton Kennel Club Show, one of many big wins for this dog owned by Mrs. H. Terrell Van Ingen. The judge is Kenneth Given.

Do not worm your dog because you "*think*" he should be wormed, or because you are advised to do so by some self-confessed "authority." Drugs employed to expel worms can prove highly dangerous to your dog if used indiscriminately and carelessly, and in many instances the same symptoms that are indicative of the presence of internal parasites can also be the signs of some other affliction.

A word here in regard to that belief that garlic will "cure" worms. Garlic is an excellent flavoring agent, favored by gourmets the world over—but—it will not rid your dog of worms. Its only curative power lies in the fact that, should you use it on a housedog who has worms, the first time he pants in your face you will definitely be cured of ever attempting this pseudo-remedy again.

ROUNDWORM

These are the most common worms found in dogs and can have great effects upon puppies, which they almost invariably infest. Potbellies, general unthriftiness, diarrhea, coughing, lack of appetite, anemia, are the symptoms. They can also cause verminous pneumonia when in the larvae stage. Fecal examination of puppy stools should be made by your veterinarian frequently if control of these parasites is to be constant. Although theoretically it is

Worms are the bane of dog breeders and owners. A cute, healthy puppy like this one can become sickly and emaciated if the deadly helminths are not eliminated.

possible for small puppies to be naturally worm free, actually most pups are born infested or contract the parasitic eggs at the mother's breast.

The roundworm lives in the intestine and feeds on the dog's partially digested food, growing and laying eggs which are passed out in the dog's stool to be picked up by him in various ways and so cause reinfestation. The life history of all the intestinal worms is a vicious circle, with the dog the beginning and the end host. This worm is yellowish-white in color and is shaped like a common garden worm, pointed at both ends. It is usually curled when found in the stool. There are several different species of this type of worm. Some varieties are more dangerous than others. They discharge toxin within the dog, and the movement of larvae to important internal sections of the dog's body can cause death.

The two drugs most used by kennel owners for the elimination of round-worms are N-butyl-chloride and tetrachloroethylene, but there are a host of other drugs, new and old, that can also do the job efficiently. With most of the worm drugs, give no food to the dog for twenty-four hours, or in the case of puppies, twenty hours, previous to the time he is given the medicine. It is absolutely essential that this starvation limit be adhered to, particularly if the drug used is tetrachloroethylene, since the existence of the slightest amount of food in the stomach or intestine can cause death. One tenth c.c. to each pound of the animal's weight is the dosage for tetrachloroethylene, followed in one hour with a milk-of-magnesia physic, *never* an oily physic. Food may be given two hours later.

N-butyl-chloride is less toxic if the dog has eaten some food during the supposed starvation period. The dosage is one c.c. for every ten pounds of the weight of the dog. Any safe physic may be administered an hour later, and the dog fed within two hours afterward. Large doses of this drug can be given grown dogs without danger, and will kill whipworms as well as roundworms. A second treatment should follow in two weeks. The effect of N-buytl-chloride is accumulative; therefore, when a large dosage is necessary, the total amount to be given can be divided into many small doses administered, one small dose at a time, over a period of hours. The object of this procedure is to prevent the dog from vomiting up the drug, which generally occurs when a large dose is given all at once. This method of administering the drug has been found to be very effective.

A new product, *piperazine*, available in several forms and marketed under various brand names, is the latest, efficient roundworm specific. It can be given in food, and eliminates the need for the starving period. In fact it will soon be sold incorporated in dog food or biscuits. Semi-annual usage in kennels could, in time, practically eliminate this scourge from dogdom.

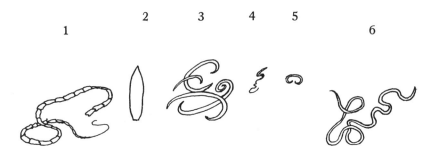

1. *Flea-host tapeworm.* 2. *Segment of tapeworm as seen in dog's stool.* 3. *Common roundworm.* 4. *Whipworm.* 5. *Hookworm.* 6. *Heartworm.*

HOOKWORMS

These tiny leeches who live on the blood of your dog, which they get from the intestinal walls, cause severe anemia, groaning, fits, diarrhea, loss of appetite and weight, rapid breathing, and swelling of the legs. The same drugs, and tolkuene, used to eradicate roundworms will also expel hookworms.

Good food is essential for quick recovery, with added amounts of liver and raw meat incorporated in the diet. Blood transfusions are often necessary if the infestation has been heavy. If one infestation follows another, a certain degree of immunity to the effects of the parasite seems to be built up by the dog. A second treatment should be given two weeks following the initial treatment.

WHIPWORMS

These small, thin whiplike worms are found in the intestines and the caecum. Those found in the intestines are reached and killed by the same drugs used in the eradication of roundworms and hookworms. Most worm medicines will kill these helminths if they reach them, but those which live in the caecum are very difficult to reach. They exude toxins which cause debilitation, anemia, and allied ills, and are probably a contributing factor in lowering the resistance to the onslaught of other infections. The usual symptoms of worm infestation are present.

N-butyl-chloride, in dosage three times greater than the roundworm dosage, appears to be quite effective in reaching the caecum and ridding the dog of most of these pests. The drug is to be given following the twenty-four hour period of fasting. Administration of an anti-emetic is generally indicated to keep the dog from disgorging the drug.

Phthalofyne is an effective whipworm eradicator that can be administered by either intravenous injection or by oral tablets.

TAPEWORMS

Tapeworms are not easily diagnosed by fecal test, but are easily identified when visible in the dog's stool. The worm is composed of two distinct parts, the head and the segmented body. It is pieces of the segmented body that we see in the stools of the dog. They are usually pink or white in color and flat. The common tapeworm, which is most prevalent in our dogs, is about eighteen inches long, and the larvae are carried by the flea. The head of the worm is smaller than a pinhead and attaches itself to the intestinal wall. Contrary to general belief, the dog infested with tapeworms does not possess an enormous appetite—rather it fluctuates from good to poor. The animal shows the general signs of worm infestation. Often he squats and drags his hindquarters on the ground. This is due to tapeworm larvae moving and wriggling in the lower bowels. One must be careful in diagnosing this symptom, as it may also mean that the dog is suffering from distended anal glands.

Author's note: There are several new medical inoculations to rid your dog, or control, external and internal parasites (fleas and the various worms). At this writing most of these drugs are in the experimental stage but, once they are found to be completely effective they will be the easy answer to this long-fought problem.

Ch. Dorey's Declared Dividend. This grand red dog is pictured here going Best Of Breed at the New England Cocker Spaniel Breeder's Club Show, 1958. He is owned by Mrs. Blanche Dorey, handled by Ted Young, Jr., and is being judged here by Mr. Clyde Heck.

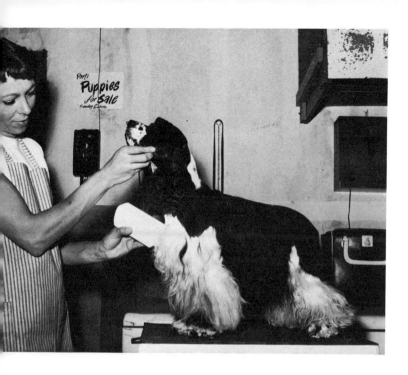

*Grooming is not just important to your Cocker's
appearance, it is also necessary to its continued
good health. Beginning skin disease can be caught
during grooming and cured before it spreads
too badly.*

Arecolene is an efficient expeller of tapeworms. Dosage is approximately
one-tenth grain for every fifteen pounds of the dog's weight, administered
after twenty hours of fasting. Nemural is also widely used. One pill for
every eight pounds of body weight is given in a small amount of food after
twelve hours of starvation. No worm medicine can be considered 100 per
cent effective in all cases. If one drug does not expel the worms satisfactorily,
then another must be tried.

HEARTWORM

This villain inhabits the heart and is the most difficult to treat. The worm
is about a foot long and literally stuffs the heart of the affected animal. It
is prevalent in the southern states and has long been the curse of sporting-dog
breeds. The worm is transmitted principally through the bite of an infected
mosquito, which can fly from an infected southern canine visitor directly
to your northern Cocker and do its dire deed.

216

Best In Show, Bucks County Kennel Club, 1960, the terrific black and tan dog, Ch. Try Cob's Spectacular, shown here being handled by Ted Young, Jr. The judge is Thomas Keator, and Mrs. H. Terrell Van Ingen is the proud owner.

The symptoms are: fatigue, gasping, coughing, nervousness, and sometimes dropsy and swelling of the extremities. Treatment for heartworms definitely must be left in the hands of your veterinarian. A wide variety of drugs are used in treatment, the most commonly employed are the arsenicals, antimony compounds, and caracide. Danger exists during cure when dying adult worms move to the lungs, causing suffocation, or when dead microfilariae, in a heavily infested dog, block the small blood vessels in the heart muscles. The invading microfilariae are not discernible in the blood until nine months following introduction of the disease by the bite of the carrier mosquito.

In an article on this subject in *Field & Stream* magazine, Joe Stetson describes a controlled experiment in which caracide was employed in periodic treatments as a preventative of heartworm. The experiment was carried out over a period of eighteen months, during which time the untreated dogs became positive for heartworm and eventually died. A post mortem proved the presence of the worm. The dogs that underwent scheduled prophylaxis

An exceptionally nice modern parti-color black and white dog, Ch. Maribeau's Master Sargent, being shown to Best Of Variety by Ted Young, Jr., at the International Kennel Club Show. The judge is Mr. Herbert Bobb, and the owner of Sargent is Mrs. Marion Bebeau. This parti was also Best In Show at the 1965 American Spaniel Club Show.

have been found, by blood test, to be free of circulating microfilariae and are thriving.

COCCIDIOSIS

This disease is caused by a single-celled protozoa. It affects dogs of all ages, but is not dangerous to mature animals. When puppies become infected by a severe case of coccidiosis, it very often proves fatal, since it produces such general weakness and emaciation that the puppy has no defense against other invading harmful organisms. Loose and bloody stools are indicative of the presence of this disease, as is loss of appetite, weakness, emaciation, discharge from the eyes, and a fever of approximately 103 degrees. The disease is contracted directly or through flies that have come from infected quarters. Infections seems to occur over and over again, limiting the puppy's chance of recovery with each succeeding infection. The duration of the disease is about three weeks, but new infestations can stretch this period of illness on until your puppy has little chance to recover. Strict sanitation and supportive treatment of good nutrition—utilizing milk, fat, kaopectate, and bone ash, with added dextrose and calcium—seem to be all that can be done in the way of treatment. Force feed the puppy if necessary. The more food that you can get into him to give him strength until the disease has run its course, the better will be his chances of recovery. Specific cures have been developed in other animals and poultry, but not as yet in dogs. Recovered dogs are life-long carriers of the disease. Sulfamethazine may give some control.

SKIN DISEASES

Diseases of the skin in dogs are many, varied, and easily confused by the kennel owner as to category. All skin afflictions should be immediately diagnosed by your veterinarian so that treatment can begin with dispatch. Whatever drug is prescribed must be employed diligently and in quantity and generally long after surface indications of the disease has ceased to exist. A surface cure may be attained, but the infection remains buried deep in the hair follicles or skin glands, to erupt again if treatment is suspended too soon. Contrary to popular belief, diet, if well balanced and complete, is seldom the cause of skin disease.

Eczema

The word "eczema" is a much-abused word, as is the word "dermatitis." Both are used with extravagance in the identification of various forms of skin disorders. We will concern ourselves with the two most prevalent forms of so-called eczema, namely wet eczema and dry eczema. In the wet form, the skin exudes moisture and then scabs over, due to constant scratching and biting by the dog at the site of infection. The dry form manifests itself in dry patches which irritate and itch, causing great discomfort to the dog. In both instances the hair falls out and the spread of the disease is rapid. The cause of these diseases is not yet known, though many are thought to be originated by various fungi and aggravated by allergic conditions. The quickest means of bringing these diseases under control is through the application of a good skin remedy often combined with a fungicide, which your veterinarian will prescribe. An over-all dip, employing specific liquid medication, is beneficial in many cases and has a continuing curative effect over a period of days. Injectable or oral anti-inflammatory drugs are supplementary treatment.

Ringworm

This infection is caused by a fungus and is highly contagious to humans. In the dog it generally appears on the face as a round or oval spot from which the hair has fallen. It is not as often seen in Cockers as it is in shorter-coated dogs. Ringworm is easily cured by the application of iodine glycerine (50 per cent of each ingredient) or a fungicide, such as girseofulvin, liberally applied.

Acne

Your puppy will frequently display small eruptions on the soft skin of his belly. These little pimples rupture and form a scab. The rash is caused by inflammation of the skin glands and is not a serious condition. Treatment consists of washing the affected area with alcohol or witch hazel, followed by the application of a healing lotion or powder. Hormonal imbalances can also cause specific skin conditions that are best left to the administrations of your veterinarian.

Hookworm Larvae Infection

The skin of your dog can become infected from the eggs and larvae of the hookworm acquired from muddy hookworm-infested runs. The larvae become stuck to his coat with mud and burrow into the skin, leaving ugly raw red patches. One or two baths in warm water to which an antiseptic has been added usually cures the condition quickly.

DEFICIENCY DISEASES

These diseases, or conditions, are caused by dietary deficiencies or some condition which robs the diet of necessary ingredients. Anemia, a deficiency condition, is a shortage of hemoglobin. Hookworms, lice, and any disease that depletes the system of red blood cells, are contributory causes. A shortage or lack of specific minerals or vitamins in the diet can also cause anemia. Not so long ago, rickets was the most common of the deficiency diseases, caused by a lack of one or more of the dietary elements—vitamin D, calcium, and phosphorus. There are other types of deficiency diseases originating

Another good one handled by Ted Young, Jr., the black and tan dog, Ch. Pinefair Plus, also owned by Mrs. H. Terrell Van Ingen. The dog is depicted going Best Of Breed at the Cocker Spaniel Club of Virginia, 1964, under judge Leslie E. Clark.

in dietary inadequacy and characterized by unthriftiness in one or more phases. The cure exists in supplying the missing food factors to the diet. Sometimes, even though all the necessary dietary elements are present in the food, some are destroyed by improper feeding procdeure. For example, a substance in raw eggs, avertin, destroys biotin, one of the B-complex group of vitamins. Cooking will destroy the avertin in the egg white and prevent a biotin deficiency in the diet.

BACTERIAL DISEASES

In this group we find leptospirosis, tetanus, pneumonia, strep infections, and many other dangerous diseases. The mortality rate is generally high in all of the bacterial diseases, and treatment should be left to your veterinarian.

Leptospirosis

Leptospirosis is spread most frequently by the urine of infected dogs, which can infect for six months or more after the animal has recovered from

Let your veterinarian arrange a series of shots for your young Cocker to protect him against the dread and deadly virus and bacterial diseases.

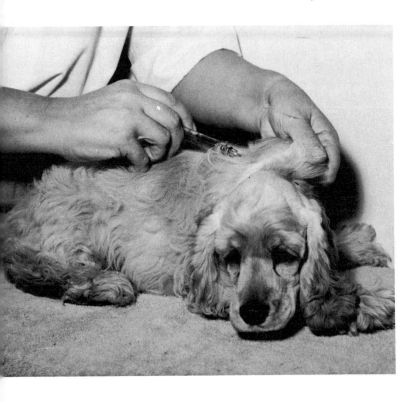

*A dog that is thrifty, a good eater, and seemingly
healthy can yet harbor the germs of deadly disease.
A periodic health check-up by your veterinarian
is a wise investment for any dog owner.*

the disease. Rats are the carriers of the bacterial agent which produces this
disease. A dog will find a bone upon which an infected rat has urinated,
chew the bone, and become infested with the disease in turn. Leptospirosis
is primarily dangerous in the damage it does to the kidneys. Complete isola-
tion of affected individuals to keep the disease from spreading and rat control
of kennel areas are the chief means of prevention. Also, Leptospirosis
vaccines may be employed by your veterinarian as a preventative measure.
Initial diagnosis is difficult, and the disease has generally made drastic inroads
before a cure is effected. It has been estimated that fully 50 per cent of all
dogs throughout the world have been stricken with leptospirosis at one time
or another and that in many instances the disease was not recognized for
what it was. The disease produced by *Leptospira* in the blood of humans is
known as Weil's disease.

Tetanus

Lockjaw bacteria produce an exceedingly deadly poison. The germs grow
in the depths of a sealed-over wound where oxygen cannot penetrate. To
prevent this disease, every deep wound acquired by your dog should be

Ch. Holly Tree High Knight, the top black dog owned by Mrs. Wm. B. Edwards, here going Best In Show at Idaho Capital City Kennel Club, 1960. The dog was handled to this fine win by Ted Young, Jr., under the capable judging of Mrs. Marie Meyer.

thoroughly cleansed and disinfected, and an antitoxin given the animal. Treatment follows the same general pattern as prevention. If the jaw locks, intravenous feeding must be given.

Strep throat

This is a very contagious disease caused by a specific group of bacteria labeled "streptococcus." Characteristic of this disease is the high temperature that accompanies infection (104 to 106 degrees). Other symptoms are loose stool at the beginning of the disease and a slight optic discharge. The throat becomes intensely inflamed, swallowing is difficult, and the glands under the ears are swollen. Immunity is developed by the host after the initial attack.

Tonsillitis

Inflammation of the tonsils can be either of bacterial or virus origin. It is not a serious disease in itself, but is often a symptom of other diseases. Tonsillitis is not to be confused with strep throat, which is produced by an entirely different organism. The symptoms of tonsillitis are enlarged and reddened tonsils, poor appetite, vomiting, and optic discharge. The disease usually runs its course in from five to seven days. Penicillin, aureomycin, terramycin, chloromycetin, etc., have been used with success in treatment.

Pneumonia

Pneumonia is a bacterial disease of the lungs of which the symptoms are poor appetite, optic discharge, shallow and rapid respiration. Affected animals become immune to the particular type of pneumonia from which they have recovered. Oral treatment utilizing antibiotic or sulfa drugs, combined with a pneumonia jacket of cloth or cotton padding wrapped around the chest area, seems to be standard treatment.

VIRUS DISEASES

The dread virus diseases are caused by the smallest organisms known to man. They live in the cells and often attack the nerve tissue. The tissue thus weakened is easily invaded by many types of bacteria. Complications then set in, and it is these accompanying ills which usually prove fatal. The secondary infections can be treated with several of the "wonder" drugs, and excellent care and nursing is necessary if the stricken animal is to survive. Your veterinarian is the only person qualified to aid your dog when a virus disease strikes. The diseases in this category include distemper, infectious hepatitis, rabies, kennel cough, and primary encephalitis—the latter actually inflammation of the brain, a condition characterizing several illnesses, particularly those of virus origin.

Distemper

Until recently a great many separate diseases had been lumped under the general heading of distemper. In the last few years modern science has isolated a number of separate diseases of the distemper complex, such as infectious hepatitis, hard-pad disease, influenza, and primary encephalitis, which had been diagnosed as distemper. Thus, with more accurate diagnosis, great strides have been made in conquering, not only distemper, but these other, allied diseases. Distemper (Carre) is no longer prevalent due to successful methods of immunization, but any signs of illness in an animal not immunized may be the beginning of the disease. The symptoms are so similar to those of various other diseases that only a trained observer can diagnose correctly. Treatment consists of the use of drugs to counteract complications arising from the invasion of secondary diseases and in keeping the stricken animal warm, well fed, comfortable and free from dehydration until the disease has run its course. In many instances, even if the dog gets well, he will be left with some dreadful souvenir of the disease which will mar him for life. After effects are common in most of the diseases of the distemper complex.

The tremendous value of immunization against this virus disease cannot be exaggerated. Except for the natural resistance your animal carries against disease, it is the one means of protection you have against this killer. There have been various methods of immunization developed in the last several years, combining several vaccines in one. The human measles vaccine

Dogs stricken with the dread virus diseases, even though they recover, are often left with some physical defect that mars them for life.

developed to protect very young puppies is highly effective. With the normal vaccine injections can be given at any age, even as early as six or eight weeks, with a repeat dosage at six months of age. It does not affect the tissues, nor can it cause any ill effects to other dogs in a kennel who come in contact with the vaccinated animal.

Infectious hepatitis

This disease attacks dogs of all ages, but is particularly deadly to puppies. We see young puppies in the nest, healthy, bright and sturdy; suddenly they begin to vomit, and the next day they are dead of infectious hepatitis—it strikes that quickly. The disease is almost impossible to diagnose correctly, and there is no known treatment that will cure it. Astute authorities claim that if an afflicted dog survives three days after the onslaught of the disease

New vaccines, new medications, are constantly being developed and researched to keep your dog healthy and long living.

he will, in all probability, completely recover. Prevention is through vaccination. Veterinarian vaccine programs usually combine distemper, hepatitis, and often leptospirosis vaccines.

Rabies

This is the most terrible of diseases, since it knows no bounds. It is transmissible to all kinds of animals and birds, including the superior animal, man. To contract this dread disease, the dog must be bitten by a rabid animal or the rabies virus must enter the body through a broken skin surface. The disease incubation period is governed by the distance of the virus point of entry to the brain. The closer the point of entry is to the brain, the quicker the disease manifests itself. We can be thankful that rabies is not nearly as prevalent as is supposed by the uninformed. Restlessness, excitability, perverted appetite, character reversal, wildness, drowsiness, loss of acuteness of senses, and of feeling in some instances, foaming at the mouth,

The fine black and tan dog, Ch. Shady Hill's Bit O'Copper, owned by Mrs. H. Terrell Van Ingen, handled by Ted Young, Jr., to Best Of Breed at the Cocker Spaniel Club Show of Rhode Island. The judge is Elwood Doyle.

*Show dogs and field trial Cockers, are constantly
exposed to disease and infection from other dogs.
Basic protection should be provided them to
minimize this danger to their health and well-being.*

and many other lesser symptoms come with the onslaught of this disease. Diagnosis by trained persons of a portion of the brain is conceded to be the only way of determining whether an animal died of rabies or of one of the distemper complex diseases. Very little has been done in introducing drugs or specifics that can give satisfaction in combatting this disease, perhaps evaluation of the efficacy of such products is almost impossible with a disease so rare and difficult to diagnose.

In 1948 an avianized, modified live virus vaccine was reported, and is being used with success. Quarantine, such as that pursued in England, even of six-months' duration, is still not the answer to the rabies question, though it is undeniably effective. It is, however, not proof positive. Recently a dog on arriving in England was held in quarantine for the usual six months. The day before he was to be released to his owners, the attendant noticed that he was acting strangely. He died the next day. Under examination his brain showed typical inclusion bodies, establishing the fact that he had died of rabies. This is a truly dangerous disease that can bring frightful death to animal or man. It should be the duty of every dog owner to protect his dog, himself, his family, and neighbors from even the slight risk that exists of contracting rabies by taking immediate advantage of immunization protection.

FITS

Fits in dogs are symptoms of diseases rather than illness itself. They can be caused by the onslaught of any number of diseases, including worms, distemper, epilepsy, primary encephalitis, poisoning, etc. Running fits can also be traced to dietary deficiencies. The underlying reason for the fits, or convulsions, must be diagnosed by your veterinarian and the cause treated.

DIARRHEA

Diarrhea, which is officially defined as watery movements occurring eight or more times a day, is often a symptom of one of many other diseases. But if, on taking your Cocker's temperature, you find there is no fever, it is quite possible the condition has been caused by either a change of diet, of climate or water, or even by a simple intestinal disturbance. A tightening agent such as kaopectate should be given. Water should be withheld and corn syrup, dissolved in boiled milk, substituted to prevent dehydration in the patient. Feed hard-boiled eggs, boiled milk, meat, cheese, boiled white rice, cracker, kibbles, or dog biscuits. Add a tablespoonful of bone ash (not bone meal) to the diet. If the condition is not corrected within two or three days, if there is an excess of blood passed in the stool, or if signs of other illness become manifest, don't delay a trip to your veterinarian.

CONSTIPATION

If the dog's stool is so hard that it is difficult for him to pass it and he strains and grunts during the process, then he is obviously constipated. The cause of constipation is one of diet. Bones and dog biscuits, given abundantly, can cause this condition, as can any of the items of diet mentioned above as treatment for diarrhea. Chronic constipation can result in hemorrhoids which, if persistent, must be removed by surgery. The cure for constipation and its accompanying ills is the introduction of laxative food elements into the diet. Stewed tomatoes, buttermilk, skim milk, whey, bran, alfalfa meal, and various fruits can be fed and a bland physic given. Enemas can bring quick relief. Once the condition is rectified, the dog should be given a good balanced diet, avoiding all types of foods that will produce constipation.

EYE AILMENTS

The eyes are not only the mirror of the soul, they are also the mirror of many kinds of disease. Discharge from the eyes is one of the many symptoms warning of most internal virus, parasitic, and bacterial diseases. Of the ailments affecting the eye itself, the most usual are: glaucoma, which seems to be a hereditary disease; pink eye, a strep infection; cataracts; opacity of the lens in older dogs; corneal opacity, such as follows some cases of infectious hepatitis; and teratoma. Mange, fungus, inturned lids, and growths on the lid are other eye ailments. The wise procedure is to consult your veterinarian for specific treatment.

When the eyes show a discharge from reasons other than those that can

A nice black dog from the coast being groomed for show and subsequent use at stud. Good health is a prime requisite in such a program.

be labeled "ailment," such as irritation from dust, wind, or sand, they should be washed with warm water on cotton or a soft cloth. After gently washing the eyes, an ophthalmic ointment combining a mild anesthetic and antiseptic can be utilized. Butyn sulphate, 1 per cent yellow oxide of mercury, and 5 per cent sulphathiazole ointment are all good. Boric acid seems to be falling out of favor as an ophthalmic antiseptic. The liquid discharged by the dog's tear ducts is a better antiseptic, and much cheaper.

ANAL GLANDS

If your dog consistently drags his rear parts on the ground or bites this area, the cause is probably impacted anal glands. These glands, which are located on each side of the anus, should be periodically cleared by squeezing. The job is not a nice one, and can be much more effectively done by your veterinarian. Unless these glands are kept reasonably clean, infection can become housed in this site, resulting in the formation of an abscess which will need surgical care. Dogs that get an abundance of exercise seldom need the anal glands attended to.

The many other ailments which your dog is heir to, such as cancer, tumors, rupture, heart disease, fractures, and the results of accidents, etc., must all be diagnosed and tended to by your veterinarian. When you go to your veterinarian with a sick dog, always remember to bring along a sample of his stool for analysis. Many times samples of his urine are needed, too. Your veterinarian is the only one qualified to treat your dog for disease,

Puppies are, of course, particularly susceptible to sickness of all kinds. The smart owner and breeder utilizes every avenue known to science to protect them.

but protection against disease is, to a great extent, in the hands of the dog's owner. If those hands are capable, a great deal of pain and misery for both dog and owner can be eliminated. Death can be cheated, investment saved, and veterinary bills kept to a minimum. A periodic health check by your veterinarian is a wise investment.

ADMINISTERING MEDICATION

Some people seem to have ten thumbs on each hand when they attempt to give medicine to their dog. They become agitated and approach the task with so little sureness that their mood is communicated to the patient increasing the difficulties presented. Invite calmness and quietness in the patient by emanating these qualities yourself. Speak to the animal in low, easy tones, petting him slowly, quieting him down in preparation. The administration of medicine should be made without fuss and as though it is some quiet and private new game between you and your dog.

At the corner of your dog's mouth there is a lip pocket perfect for the administering of liquid medicine if used correctly. Have the animal sit, then raise his muzzle so that his head is slanted upward looking toward the sky. Slide two fingers in the corner of his mouth where the upper and lower lip edges join, pull gently outward, and you have a pocket between the cheek flesh and the gums. Into this pocket pour the liquid medicine slowly. Keep his head up, and the liquid will run from the pocket into his throat and he will swallow it. Continue this procedure until the complete dose has been given. This will be easier to accomplish if the medicine has been spooned into a small bottle. The bottle neck, inserted into the lip pocket, is tipped, and the contents drained slowly down the dog's throat.

To give pills or capsules, the head of the patient must again be raised with muzzle pointing upward. With one hand, grasp the cheeks of the dog just behind the lip edges where the teeth come together on the inside of the mouth. With the thumb on one side and the fingers on the other, press inward as though squeezing. The lips are pushed against the teeth, and the pressure of your fingers forces the mouth open. The dog will not completely close his mouth, since doing so would cause him to bite his lip. With your other hand, insert the pill in the patient's mouth as far back on the base of the tongue as you can, pushing it back with your second finger. Withdraw your hand quickly, allow the dog to close his mouth, and hold it closed with your hand, but not too tightly. Massage the dog's throat and watch for the tip of his tongue to show between his front teeth, signifying the fact that the capsule or pill has been swallowed.

In taking your dog's temperature, an ordinary rectal thermometer is adequate. It must be first shaken down, then dipped in vaseline, and inserted into the rectum for approximately three-quarters of its length. Allow it to remain there for no less than a full minute, restraining the dog from sitting completely during that time. When withdrawn, it should be wiped with a piece of cotton, read, then washed in alcohol—never hot water. The arrow on most thermometers at 98.6 degrees indicates normal human temperature and should be disregarded. Normal temperature for your own dog is 101 degrees; normal puppy temperature varies between $101\frac{1}{2}$ to 102 degrees. Excitement can raise the temperature, so it is best to take a reading only after the dog is calm.

In applying an ophthalmic ointment to the eye, simply pull the lower lid out, squeeze a small amount of ointment into the pocket thus produced,

and release the lid. The dog will blink, and the ointment will spread over the eye.

Should you find it necessary to give your dog an enema, employ an ordinary human-size bag and rubber hose. Simply grease the catheter with vaseline and insert the hose well into the rectum. The bag should be held high for a constant flow of water. Warm soapy water or plain water with a tablespoonful of salt makes an efficient enema.

FIRST AID

Emergencies quite frequently occur which make it necessary for you to care for the dog yourself until veterinary aid is available. Quite often emergency help by the owner can save the dog's life or lessen the chance of permanent injury. A badly injured animal, blinded to all else but abysmal pain, often reverts to the primitive wanting only to be left alone with his misery. Injured, panic-stricken, not recognizing you, he might attempt to

234

In 1952 the handsome black and tan, Ch. Bigg's Believe It Or Not, went Best In Show at the American Spaniel Club Show. This is a photographic record of that win. The dog is owned by Mr. Robert W. Biggs, and was handled to this good win by Ted Young, Jr., under judge, Mrs. Hartley Dodge.

bite when you wish to help him. Under the stress of fright and pain, this reaction is normal in animals. A muzzle can easily be slipped over his foreface, or a piece of bandage or strip of cloth can be fashioned into a muzzle by looping it around the dog's muzzle, crossing it under the jaws, and bringing the two ends around in back of the dog's head and tying them. Snap a leash onto his collar as quickly as possible to prevent him from running away and hiding. If it is necessary to lift him, grasp him by the neck, getting as large a handful of skin as you can, as high up on the neck as possible. Hold tight and he won't be able to turn his head far enough around to bite. Lift him by the hold you have on his neck until he is far enough off the ground to enable you to encircle his body with your other arm and support him or carry him.

Every dog owner should have handy a first-aid kit specifically for the use of his dog. It should contain a thermometer, surgical scissors, rolls of three-inch and six-inch bandage, a roll of one-inch adhesive tape, a package of surgical cotton, a jar of vaseline, enema equipment, bulb syringe, ten c.c.

hypodermic syringe, flea powder, skin remedy, tweezers, ophthalmic ointment, paregoric, kaopectate, peroxide of hydrogen, merthiolate, army formula foot powder, alcohol, ear remedy, aspirin, milk of magnesia, castor oil, mineral oil, dressing salve.

We have prepared two charts for your reference, one covering general first-aid measures and the other a chart of poisons and antidotes. Remember that, in most instances, these are emergency measures, not specific treatments, and are designed to help you in aiding your dog until you can reach your veterinarian.

FIRST-AID CHART

Emergency	Treatment	Remarks
Accidents	Automobile, Treat for shock. If gums are white, indicates probable internal injury. Wrap bandage tightly around body until it forms a sheath. Keep very quiet until veterinarian comes.	Call veterinarian immediately.
Bee stings	Give paregoric, 1 teaspoonful, or aspirin to ease pain. If in state of shock, treat for same.	Call veterinarian for advice.
Bites (animal)	Tooth wounds—area should be shaved and antiseptic solution flowed into punctures with eye dropper. Iodine, merthiolate, etc., can be used. If badly bitten or ripped, take dog to your veterinarian for treatment.	If superficial wounds become infected after first aid, consult veterinarian.
Bloat	Stomach distends like a balloon. Pierce stomach wall with hollow needle to allow gas to escape. Follow with stimulant—2 cups of coffee. Then treat for shock.	
Burns	Apply strong, strained tea to burned area, followed by covering of vaseline.	Unless burn is very minor, consult veterinarian immediately.
Broken bones	If break involves a limb, fashion splint to keep immobile. If ribs, pelvis, shoulder, or back involved, keep dog from moving until professional help comes.	Call veterinarian immediately.
Choking	If bone, wood, or any foreign object can be seen at back of mouth or throat, remove with fingers. If object can't be removed or is too deeply imbedded or too far back in throat, rush to veterinarian immediately.	

236

The sign tells the story of this nice win for Abbi's
Adored Mister A.O.K. The judge is Mrs. Edna
Joel and the dog is handled by his owner,
Mrs. Harry Reno.

Cuts	Minor cuts: allow dog to lick and cleanse. If not within his reach, clean cut with peroxide, then apply merthiolate. Severe cuts: apply pressure bandage to stop bleeding—a wad of bandage over wound and bandage wrapped tightly over it. Take to veterinarian.	If cut becomes infected or needs suturing, consult veterinarian. (*see* TETANUS).
Dislocations	Keep dog quiet and take to veterinarian at once.	
Drowning	Artificial respiration. Lay dog on his side, push with hand on his ribs, release quickly. Repeat every 2 seconds. Treat for shock.	New method of artificial respiration as employed by fire department useful here.
Electric shock	Artificial respiration. Treat for shock.	Call veterinarian immediately.

An informal portrait by Liz, the fine animal photographer, of a pair of nice partis in a rather compromising pose.

Heat stroke	Quickly immerse the dog in cold water until relief is given. Give cold water enema. Or lay dog flat and pour cold water over him, turn electric fan on him, and continue pouring cold water as it evaporates.	Cold towel pressed against abdomen aids in reducing temp. quickly if quantity of water not available.
Porcupine quills	Tie dog up, hold him between knees, and pull all quills out with pliers. Don't forget tongue and inside of mouth.	See veterinarian to remove quills too deeply imbedded.
Shock	Cover dog with blanket. Administer stimulant (coffee with sugar). Allow him to rest, and soothe with voice and hand.	Alcoholic beverages are NOT a stimulant.
Snake bite	Cut deep X over fang marks. Drop potassium-permanganate into cut. Apply tourniquet above bite if on leg.	Apply first aid only if a veterinarian or a doctor can't be reached.

Children get a tremendous kick out of handling their own dog. The Cocker is just the right size for the budding handler.

Best In Show in 1964 at the Greenwich Kennel Club Show, went to the grand silver buff dog, Ch. Bigg's Snow Prince, a great winner in the breed. The judge at this event was Mrs. Matthew Imrie. The dog is owned by Mrs. H. Terrell Van Ingen, and was handled by Ted Young, Jr.

The important thing to remember when your dog is poisoned is that prompt action is imperative. Administer an emetic immediately. Mix hydrogen peroxide and water in equal parts. Force two to four tablespoonfuls of this mixture down your dog. In a few minutes he will regurgitate his stomach contents. Once this has been accomplished, call your veterinarian. If you know the source of the poison and the container which it came from is handy, you will find the antidote on the label. Your veterinarian will prescribe specific drugs and advise on their use.

The symptoms of poisoning include trembling, panting, intestinal pain, vomiting, slimy secretion from mouth, convulsions, coma. All these symptoms are also prevalent in other illnesses, but if they appear and investigation leads you to believe that they are the result of poisoning, act with dispatch as described before.

Show business personalities are inevitably attracted to the winsome beauty of the Cocker Spaniel. Here is Patti Page enchanted by a soft and cuddly Cocker puppy.

POISON	HOUSEHOLD ANTIDOTE
ACIDS	Bicarbonate of soda
ALKALIES	Vinegar or lemon juice
(cleansing agents)	
ARSENIC	Epsom salts
HYDROCYANIC ACID	Dextrose or corn sirup
(wild cherry; laurel leaves)	
LEAD	Epsom salts
(paint pigments)	
PHOSPHORUS	Peroxide of hydrogen
(rat poison)	
MERCURY	Eggs and milk
THEOBROMINE	Phenobarbital
(cooking chocolate)	
THALLIUM	Table salt in water
(bug poisons)	
FOOD POISONING	Peroxide of hydrogen, followed by enema
(garbage, etc.)	
STRYCHNINE	Sedatives. Phenobarbital, Nembutal.
DDT	Peroxide and enema.

Ch. Benfield's Champagne Snow Cap, the silver buff dog owned by the Duffield Hamiltons, is being handled here by Ted Young to a well-deserved win, Best Of Variety, Trenton Kennel Club, 1966. This fine Cocker was put up at this event by judge, Mrs. Rose Robbins.

XV

The Future of the
Cocker Spaniel

What does the future hold for the Cocker Spaniel? We are not seers so we cannot predict the future with any degree of accuracy. We can only review what has gone before and refrain from repeating the mistakes of the past or present and so attempt to find advancement in the time to come. We can advance our own theories in reference to the breed, but they must come from knowledge and objective thought, not arrogance. We must remember that no matter how perfect the dog of the present may be there is always room for improvement in some important aspect of the breed.

We have seen changes in type toward definite ideals and have seen those ideals discarded when the end result was not wholly satisfactory. We have seen the successful results of intelligent breeding programs nullified when the valuable stock of such programs fell into the wrong hands and greed or unthinking, careless subsequent breeding lost to the breed valuable genetic material. We have seen "kennel blindness" and the worship of titles or "tags" result in the production of worthless animals. And we have seen valuable breeding stock overlooked and lost to the future in favor of more glamorous contemporaries whose value may or may not have been as great. And, to the credit of the breeders, we have also seen dogs who were not successful show champions, used for the definite betterment of the breed.

This recognition of great dogs, which has occurred several times in Cocker history is, in all probability, not equalled in any other breed. We know that it is not always the great, well advertised, popular winner that is the best producer for the future. Yet, in most breeds, such animals are inevitably selected to fill that important niche. It will ever be a monument to the good sense and sure knowledge of Cocker breeders and the Cocker fancy that such dogs as Obo, Red Brucie and Torohill Trader, as well as the many other dogs of slightly lesser merit, were recognized for what they were and their great genetic worth incorporated strongly in the breed.

There has been a relatively steady climb toward greater beauty and utility based on good sense and good breeding practice, and the ever increasing interest in the Cocker as a gun dog is the sign of a healthy and diversified fancy. To this latter area of endeavor the Cocker fancy should give more than lip service. When fanciers of a breed are fortunate enough to find a definite utilitarian purpose for their animals it should not be overlooked or given only half-hearted support. The Cocker Spaniel is a sporting dog and this we must never forget. As a pet, in the show ring, the Cocker can equal any breed, but there is no other breed of dog that can be called the smallest of the gundogs, and in this he is unique. Take the Cocker out of the field and you rob him of his heritage and his specialized abilities. The Cocker can be a pet, show dog and gun dog, and in all three areas be superb. He can be only one, or two, or a combination of all three of these things and in each instance give complete satisfaction to his owner. Truly, the Cocker is a "Jack-of-all-trades" but, if you please, master of all, too.

In the final analysis the future of the Cocker Spaniel is up to you, the owners and breeders. You must carry the responsibility for molding the future of the breed. Face the future with open minds and with tolerance. Learn to understand the many new concepts in care, medicine and breeding that will be a part of the future and avoid harking back blindly to the incomplete knowledge of the past. It is our job to take the new tools that new knowledge will fashion for us and use them well. And we must never forget that a small, easily kept, hardy sporting dog that can do his job well in the field, will always be popular.

In you, the breeder, is vested the power to fashion heredity to mold life in this Cocker breed. You can and, as a breeder, will use this power that creates life and change, that brings special life-forms into being. You can design a pattern of heredity. To do it well, to mold a worthwhile pattern, you must be aware of the power you have and the intelligence to use it well. If the future is to give you what you want for the breed, then you must clear your mind of inaccuracy and absorb truth instead. This then, is the future; a time when yesterday's miracles become today's facts through science and experimentation.

What has gone before has shaped the breed as we know it now. What is done now with the breed will shape it's future. It is up to you.

The End

Glossary of Field Trial and Hunting Terminology

Bevy: A flock of birds.

Birdy: A dog with strong bird-hunting instinct.

Blind: The place, man-made or natural, that the hunter utilizes as cover.

Brace: Two dogs (a matched pair).

Break: Failure to stop at flush, shot or command.

Broken Color: Solid color broken by patches of another color.

Bye: In a field-trial the odd dog left after braces are drawn.

Coupling: A leash or ring for holding two dogs together.

Decoy: Mock bird (waterfowl) used to lure birds of like species to gun.

Derby: Field-trial competition for young, novice sporting dogs.

Delivery: The act of surrendering retrieved game (or object) to handler.

Drawing: Selection by lots of dogs to be run in pairs in field-trial stake.

Dummy: Object used to teach dog to retrieve.

Fetch: To retrieve and return downed game (or object) to handler.

Field Trial: Competition for sporting dogs which is judged for the breed's specific ability.

Flush: To drive birds from cover.

Futurity Stakes: A class at field-trials (or dog shows) for young dogs which have been nominated before birth.

Game: Prey or hunted quarry.

Gun dog: A dog that is trained to work to the gun.

Guns: The men (or women) who shoot the flushed game at field trials.

Gun-shy: A dog who fears sound and sight of the gun.

Hard-mouthed: A dog who injures or marks the game in retrieve.

Hie on: A hunting command to urge the dog on (in hunting or field-trials).

Hound marked: A three-color dog, white, tan and black.

Hup: Command given to gun dogs to sit (as at flush or shot).

Leather: Ears.

Mark: Pinpointing the spot where game fell so direct retrieve can be made.

Mute: To trail game without baying or barking.

Potterer: A dog that is slow (and sometimes unsure) on scent.

Quarter: The process by which the dog works the field ahead of the gun.

Retrieve: The act of finding and returning shot game to handler.

Runner: A shot bird that runs through cover to escape.

Scent: The odor left by an animal in passing, on ground or in the air.

Soft-mouthed: A dog (usually a puppy) who constantly drops its birds.

Spring: (Same as "Flush").

Stake: In field-trial competition, the designation of a class.

Stern: Tail (also rudder).

Team: Three or more dogs (usually four).

Tender-mouthed: A dog who handles game correctly without damage to it.

The Fall: Where a shot bird came down.

Trail: To hunt by following scent left on ground by game or quarry.

Wing-clipped: A bird not wounded but unable to fly due to shot through wing feathers.

Glossary of Genetic Terms

1. GENE (noun; adj. genotypic). A single unit of inheritance (Mendel's "Determiners"); a microscopic part of a chromosome.

2. CHROMOSOMES (noun; adj. autosomal). Small microscopic bodies within the cells of all living things. When division of cells begins the chromosomes appear as short strings of beads or rods.

3. DOMINANT (adj.). A trait or character that is seen. Indicates that a trait contributed by one parent conceals that from the other parent. For example, dark eyes are dominant over light eyes.

4. RECESSIVE (adj.). A trait or character that is concealed by a like dominant character. Exception: when no dominant is present and recessive genes pair for a certain trait. Paired recessives = Visibility.

5. FACTOR (noun). A simple Mendelian trait: may be considered synonymous with gene.

6. HETEROZYGOUS (adj.). Possessing contrasting genes (or allelomorphs). Where dominant and recessive genes are both present for any trait or traits.

7. HOMOZYGOUS (adj.). Pure for a given trait, or possessing matched genes for that trait. The opposite of heterozygous. (Thus inbred strains are said to be homozygous, and out-crossed animals to be heterozygous. Degree must be substantiated).

8. GENOTYPE (noun; adj. genotypic). The hereditary composition of an individual. The sum total of every animal's dominant and recessive traits.

9. PHENOTYPE (noun: adj. phenotypic). The external appearance of an individual. The outward manifestation of all dominant genetic material (or double recessive. See Recessive).

10. ALLELOMORPHS (noun; adj. allelomorphic). Genes, factors, traits or types which segregate as alternatives. Contrasting gene pattern.

11. ALLELE (noun). A gene, factor, trait, which differs from its sister gene. See Allelomorph.

12. AUTOSOMES (noun; adj. autosomal). Paired, ordinary chromosomes, similar in both sexes, as differentiated from the sex chromosomes.

13. CROSSING-OVER (noun). An exchange of inheritance factors or genes between related chromosomes.

14. HYPOSTASIS (noun; adj. hypostatic). The masking of the effect of another factor, not an allelomorph. For example, the masking of the ticking factor in dogs by solid color.

15. EPISTASIS (noun; adj. epistatic). Similar to hypostasis. Like dominance but epistasis occurs between factors not alternative or allelomorphic.

16. ♂ Indicates a male. The symbol represents the shield and spear of Mars, the God of War.

17. ♀ Indicates a female. This symbol represents the mirror of the Goddess of Love, Venus.

18. × Means "with", "between", etc. A mating between any male and female, .

19. F_1 Represents the first filial generation. The progeny or "get" produced from any specific mating.

20. F_2 Is the symbol used to denote the second filial generation, that is, the progeny, or young, produced from a mating of a male and female from the F_1 breeding above.

21. GET. Puppies or offspring.

Bibliography

Arenas, N., and Sammartino, R., *"Le Cycle Sexuel de la Chienne." Etude. Histol. Bull. Histol. Appl. Physiol. et Path.*, 16:299 (1939).

Ash, E. C., *Dogs: Their History and Development*, 2 vols., London, 1927.

Anrep, G. V., "Pitch Discrimination in the Dog." *J. Physiol.*, 53:376–85 (1920).

Barrows, W. M., *Science of Animal Life*. New York, World Book Co., 1927.

Burns, Marca, 1952. The Genetics of the Dog, Comm. Agri. Bur., Eng. 122 pp.

Castle, W. E., *Genetics and Eugenics*, 4th ed. Cambridge, Mass., Harvard University Press, 1930.

Darwin, C., *The Variation of Animals and Plants Under Domestication*, New York, D. Appleton Co., 1890.

Davenport, C. B., *Heredity in Relation to Eugenics*. New York, Henry Holt & Co., Inc., 1911.

Dorland, W. A. N., A.M., M.D., F.A.C.S., *The American Illustrated Medical Dictionary*. Philadelphia, W. B. Saunders Co., 1938.

Duncan, W. C., *Dog Training Made Easy*. Boston, Little, Brown & Co., 1940.

Dunn, L. C., and Dobzhansky, T., *Heredity, Race and Society*. New York, New American Library of World Literature, 1946.

Elliot, David D., *Training Gun Dogs to Retrieve*. New York, Henry Holt & Co., 1952.

Evans, H. M., and Cole, H. H., "An Introduction to the Study of the Oestrus Cycle of the Dog." *Mem. Univ. Cal.*, Vol. 9, No. 2.

Hart, E. H., "Artificial Insemination." *Your Dog* (March, 1948).

—— "The Judging Situation." *Your Dog* (March 1948).

—— 1950. Doggy Hints. Men Mg. Zenith Pub. Co.

—— *This is the Puppy*, T.F.H. Publications, Inc., 1962.

—— *Budgerigar Handbook*, T.F.H. Publications, Inc., 1960.

—— *This is the Weimaraner*, T.F.H. Publications, Inc., 1965.

—— *Your Poodle Puppy*, T.F.H. Publications, Inc., 1966.

—— and Goldbecker, *This is the German Shepherd*, T.F.H. Publications, Inc., 1955.

Hermansson, K. A., "Artificial Impregnation of the Dog." *Svensk. Vet. Tidshr.*, 39:382 (1934).

Humphrey, E. S., Articles. *The Bulletin Shep. Dog Cl. of Amer.* (1923–1927).

—— "Mental Tests for Shepherd Dogs." *J. of Hered.*, 25:129 (1934).

—— and Warner, Lucien, *Working Dogs*. Baltimore, Johns Hopkins Press, 1934.

Keeler, C. E., and Trimble, H. C., "Inheritance of Dewclaws." *J. of Hered.*, 29:145 (1938).

Kelly, G. L., and Whitney, L. F., Prevention of Conception in Bitches by Injections of Estrone. *J. Ga. Med. Assoc.*, 29:7 (1940).

Kraus, C., *"Beitrag zum Prostatakrebs und Kryptorchismus des Hundes." Frankfurter Zeitsch. Path.*, 41:405 (1931).

Krushinsky, L. A., "A Study of the Phenogenetics of Behavior Characters in Dogs." *Biol. Journ. T.*, VII, No. 4, Inst. Zool., Moscow State Univ. 1938).

Laughlin, H. H., "Racing Capacity of Horses." Dept. of Genetics 37–73. Yearbook, Carn. Inst., No. 30, *The Blood Horse*, 1931.

MacDowell, E. C., "Heredity of Behaviour in Dogs." Dept. of Genetics. *Yearbook*, Carn. Inst.

Moffit, E. B., The Cocker Spaniel, Orange Judd Co., Inc. N.Y., 1935.

Nagel, W. A., *Der Farbensinn des Hundes. Zbl. Physiol.*, 21 (1907).

Pearson, K., and Usher, C. H., "Albinism in Dogs." *Biometrica*, 21:144–163 (1929).

Razran, H. S., and Warden, C. J., "The Sensory Capacities of the Dog (Russian Schools)." *Psychol. Bulletin* 26, 1929.

Thorburn, Shooting Directory, 1805.

Stetson, J., "Heartworm Can Be Controlled." *Field and Stream* (June 1954).

Telever, J., 1934. When Is the Heat Period of the Dog?

Whitney, L. F., *The Basis of Breeding*. N. H. Fowler, 1928.

—— *How to Breed Dogs*. New York, Orange Judd Pub. Co., 1947.

—— *Feeding Our Dogs*. New York, D. van Nostrand Co., Inc., 1949.

—— *Complete Book of Dog Care*. Garden City, L.I., Doubleday & Co., Inc., 1953.

—— and Whitney, G. D., *The Distemper Complex*. Orange, Conn., Practical Science Pub. Co., 1953.

Index

Steadiness, 178
Sterility, 124
Stetson, Joe, 217
Stilbestrol, 116
Stonehenge, 28
Strep Infections, 222
Strep Throat, 224
Streptococcus, 224, 225
Stud Dog, 119, 120
Stud Dog, Care of, 119
Stylish Pride, 27
Sulfa Drugs, 225
Sulfamethazine, 219
Sulphathiazole Ointment, 231
Supplement, 68, 69, 72, 105
Sussex Spaniel, 11, 27
Sweet Georgia Brown, 22

T

Table, Grooming, 160
Table Scraps, 72
Tail Docking, 114, 129
Tan, 12
Tapeworm, 213
Tartar, 93
Ted Obo, 18
Teeth, 93, 141
Telegony, 34
Temperament, 50, 57
Temperature, 233
Terramycin, 225
Tetanus, 222, 223, 224
Tetrachloroethylene, 211
The Great My Own, 22
The Origin of Species, 33
Thorburn, 26
Ticks, 204, 205
Tidbit, 164
Tie, 120, 124
Tim Obo, 18
Tolkuene, 212
Tomarctus, 9
Tonsilitis, 225
Torohill Smokey, 24
Torohill Tidy, 22
Torohill Trader, 22, 24, 245
Torohill Trouper, 22
Toy Spaniel, 11

"Trader" Type, 26
Trainers, Professional, 178, 185
Training, 143, 148, 153, 154, 160,
    162, 165, 179
Training Classes, 143
Training, Field, 185
Training, Initial, 151
Training, Initial Essentials, 185
Training, For the Show Ring, 157, 159
Training Techniques, 146
Traveling, 94
Tricolor, 42
Trimming, 162

U

Undercoat, 91
Uniformity, 58

V

Vail, Elias, 31
Veterinarian, 201, 202
Vigor, 50, 57
Virus Diseases, 225
Vitamins, 66, 68

W

Warner, Mrs., 18
Water, 73, 78, 151
"Water" Spaniel, 11
Water Work, 181
Watson, James, 12, 16
Weaning, 130
Weil's Disease, 223
Westminster Kennel Club, 11, 22, 24
Whelping, 107, 108, 110, 111
Whelping Box, 106, 107
Whipworm, 212
Whistle, 180, 181
White, 42, 44
Whitney, Dr. Leon F., 52
Willey, Mr. J. P., 15
Windsweep Kennels, 21
Woodland Flossie, 18
Woodland Queen, 18
Worms, 130, 207, 210
Worming, 210

Y

Yellow Oxide of Mercury, 231